ROBESPIERRE

ROBESPIERRE BEFORE THE CONVENTION

(From a contemporary engraving)

ROBESPIERRE

BY

G. J. RENIER, Ph.D.

M

D. APPLETON-CENTURY COMPANY

INCORPORATED

NEW YORK   LONDON

1936

B
R55T

CONTENTS

ROBESPIERRE

I

THE PROBLEM

*Robespierre ne sera jamais bien connu
par l'histoire.* Napoleon.

Students of the life of Maximilien Robespierre, revolutionary, dictator, and terrorist, have found it difficult to agree upon the main facts, impossible to reach common conclusions as to his personality, the motives of his actions, and their interpretation.

To the enemies of the French Revolution Robespierre represents the Revolution at its worst. To its admirers he is the most glorious embodiment of all the ideals for which it stood, or else the scapegoat upon which is loaded the responsibility for what was admittedly wrong in a period when human life was held cheap. He has been depicted in turn as a saint, a hero, a villain, a degenerate, a psychopath, a far-seeing leader of the social revolution. French authors of the twentieth century have written about him with the devotion or the hatred of contemporaries.

1

It is difficult, well-nigh impossible, for a Frenchman not to be either for or against the Revolution. The European who is a friend of France but the slave of no formula may approach the problem of Robespierre with less obvious partisanship. He cannot, of course, genuinely imagine himself to be so free from preconceived notions that his verdict will be at once final and universally valid.

Let me try, therefore, to make clear in the first place what aspect of the life of Robespierre has drawn me towards his personality and time; what is the creed, however negative, that has directed and warped my judgment.

Our own period is familiar with revolutions. Ever since the end of the first decade of the twentieth century Europe has contemplated pictures of violence, in the respectable shape of war, or in the shape of revolution, respectable only in the case of success. War and revolution have bred dictatorships, erratic and unclean in their methods, based upon two fundamental untruths: that some human mind can hold the monopoly of wisdom and of righteousness, and that human beings can be mere instruments at the disposal of a mastermind. Those who have become infected with these beliefs, so alien to the principles of freedom and human dignity for which our Western-European ancestors have fought, turn towards the past and its distant stories of dictators and tyrants, less for guidance than for justification. Patient history can be made to justify any thesis, any aberration. Germany pours out biographies of Oliver Cromwell. Italy gazes upon the Caesars of ancient Rome. Soviet Russia and her disciples draw comparisons between Commissars and Conventionnels.

Those of us, however, who still hold with the gentler methods of persuasion, with the broad humanity of free debate, with serene toleration and the statelier methods of empirical meliorism, also turn towards the revolutions and dictatorships of the past. We search their records for information about the vagaries of human beings placed in situations not unlike those of the living present, and equally burdened with idealism and fear.

At the risk of being found wanting in idealism I must confess to a disbelief in the efficacy of revolutions. It is based upon my lack of trust in the light of human reason. England has known a revolution which established a short-lived commonwealth, and a

3

minor upheaval, known by the courtesy name of 'Glorious Revolution,' which was lasting in its effect because it was bloodless, reasonable and eminently irrational. The Russian Revolution was not a revolution at all. Men endowed with energy and a doctrine stepped into a vacuum and imposed their will upon a notoriously backboneless people. The great French Revolution, as has often been said, devoured its own children, was turned into a military dictatorship, and ended, in 1815, in a limited monarchy of the kind that had been reached by agreement as early as 1790.

Indeed, revolutions make very little difference in the march of human events. They affect the life of one or two generations, and either culminate in changes that would have been brought about in any case by the sheer force of economic and intellectual factors, or else lead to their antithesis, a consolidation of the situation they have attempted to overthrow. The discomforts, the sufferings of contemporaries, their dreams and their endeavours, their ideals and sacrifices are soon forgotten. They are superficial shivers on the skin of the vast collective animal that ambles on with slow but steady gait.

Free choice is as illusory in history as it is vital in politics. Supreme value in ethics, the individual hardly matters to history. The epic quality of the French Revolution resides not in its noted men but in its masses, in the heroism of the anonymous ones who fought and died at the front, in the magnificent hideousness of its mobs, so strangely unanimous in their frenzies, never flat or dull in the expression of their likes and their dislikes. It resides in the amazing collective hallucination of men who believed that a new dawn had suddenly broken, and that the faithful repetition of the formula 'freedom, equality, brotherhood' would usher in a period of happiness for the votaries of the new creed, and for all those whom they could convert by persuasion or violence.

As for the great men of the period,—a period which, from the point of view of European history, stretches from 1789 to the return of the Bourbons—there are three of them, and three only, who tower above their contemporaries. These three were self-seekers, men who wrenched themselves loose from the collective movement that inspired the others. There was Fouché, cad, scoundrel, psychologist of genius. There was Talleyrand, a plausible rogue, so clever that he turned emperors into playthings. There was Napoleon, topographer and bully, endowed with a memory more valuable than intelligence or inspiration. These men, for a brief while, moulded the world in their hands. All other men were puny. Tossed by the waves of circumstance, they rose to the crest and were sucked down into the whirlpool, or, deflated, became the flotsam of history. Those whom the waves lifted highest were those who had least substance. They were theories invested with flesh, passions and fears hidden behind man-like masks. Of the puppets whose names we remember, the most memorable is Maximilien Robespierre, the man with the infinite variety of posthumous reputations.[1]

---

[1] The terms 'conservative,' 'liberal,' 'radical,' 'socialist,' have been used throughout in their present-day meaning.

II

THE MAN

Maximilien de Robespierre was born at Arras on May 6, 1758. There is no need to enquire into the distant origins of his family, into his alleged Irish ancestry, into the theories that make him, alternatively, descend from the Rouvespieres who were settled in Flanders as early as the fifteenth century. Neither are we required to conjure up the dark streets of old Arras, the flat vistas of the province of Artois, part of the Flemish plain, or to meditate upon the fact that de Robespierre belonged to a population for which the Burgundian tradition had been a reality, a population which had given to the world men like Rubens and the Van Arteveldes. The part heredity plays in the shaping of men is a mystery. As for theories of environmental and regional influence, attractive though they may seem, and useful though local patriotism can be as an antidote to nationalism, they fail to explain the diversity of human types that spring from

even the most restricted area. Some of the
de Robespierres went one way, Maximilien
went another. Provided their blood is not
tainted, men would appear to start from
scratch.

What matters about the family history of
the de Robespierres is that they had been
lawyers for generations. This fact determined
Maximilien's choice of a career. His father
was a barrister at Arras, and so had been his
grandfather. But his father married below his
status, and his mother had no fortune. She
was the daughter of a brewer, in a country
and at a time when brewing was not synony-
mous with wealth. The marriage was a love
match and somewhat precipitate: Maximilien
made his entrance into the world less than
five months afterwards.

Were we in possession of copious details,
Maximilien's childhood might deserve close
study. Would it not enable us to understand
why the system of education that was shared
by so many of his compatriots, why the reading
of authors familiar to all the cultivated French
and to many foreigners of his age, should have
influenced him in the way they did, and distinguished him from the mass? We must

resign ourselves to the acceptance of the fact that his temperament was peculiar. How peculiar the story of his life will show. More than peculiar, however, it was not. Maximilien was not a pathological case.

In what we know of his childhood there is nothing that need have made him fundamentally different from other people. He was brought up at home by his mother, till he lost her when he was seven years of age. His father died three years later. A brother, younger than he, and two sisters, survived. At the death of the mother, the girls were sent to a convent school, and Maximilien to the Collège (the grammar school) of Arras. His maternal grandparents looked after his education, and he spent his holidays and free Sundays with them. In their house he kept his pet birds, sparrows and pigeons, of which he was very fond. He does not appear to have stood apart from other children, but he was an excellent pupil and soon at the top of his form.

At the age of eleven Maximilien was granted a scholarship which enabled him to go to the Collège Louis-le-Grand, in Paris. It was the best school in France. Formerly run by Jesuits, it had become part of the University of Paris when their Order was dissolved in 1762. A number of the masters were still ecclesiastics who had belonged to the Society of Jesus. Among the ex-pupils of Louis-le-Grand were famous and notorious men. Ten years before Maximilien de Robespierre, the Marquis de Sade had sat on its benches. In this establishment Maximilien's mind was shaped by the severe and formal training through which most of the leading spirits of the age had to pass. He learned Greek and the history of Greece, Latin almost as a living language, and Roman history as though every detail of it still vitally mattered. Modern literature was studied mainly in the classics of the seventeenth century, and of these he enjoyed Racine most. Then followed rhetoric, taught on the principle that truth was invariably communicable by word of mouth, provided it were expressed with clearness and a number of subdivisions. The eloquent man was *vir bonus dicendi peritus,* Cicero was his model. Philosophy came next, which was mainly the logic of the schools. It made truth as easy to discern as rhetoric made it easy to convey. At the basis of this system of instruction lay the French pride in clearness, the clearness of the language of France, the clearness and infallibility of its thought. 'What is not clear is not French,' said Rivarol. Nothing existed but what was within man's ken, and all that existed could be poured into the mould of irrefutable syllogisms. And if, even from the clerical masters, no excess of religious tuition was to be expected—for was it not the century of enlightenment?—all that was of importance for determining the conduct of men could be known through reason and had, *ipso facto*, been formulated long ago by the ancients.

Into this scheme of studies young de Robespierre threw himself with conviction and ardour. He was at no time half-hearted, never inclined to take his ease. Republican Rome became endowed for him with a tangible reality. Virtue lived in its steel-souled men who died for a principle and never swerved from the path of duty. His Rome was innocent of the technicalities of classical learning. He remained unaware of the fact that the loyalties of his ancient heroes, the fatherland that was for ever on their lips, were restricted to a narrow class, that the mass of slaves never, the plebs hardly, shared their religious and spiritual inheritance. He took prizes in Latin themes and

Latin versions; his efforts in French composition were outstanding, but Roman history found him at his best. In the top form, his master dubbed him 'the Roman.' So undeniably was he the best pupil of the school that when the new King Louis XVI, on his return from being anointed at Rheims, in 1774, honoured the college with a visit, young de Robespierre was entrusted with the awe-inspiring honour of reading the Latin address of welcome to His Majesty.

The most contradictory accounts have been left by Maximilien's fellow-pupils. He has been described as morose and unsociable, as popular and gay. Some, no doubt, attributed to the boy the qualities or defects they read in him as an adult. But even the contradictory reminiscences are not entirely incompatible. We can imagine Maximilien to have been moody and sensitive, elated at one moment by a success in the class-room, dejected or even resentful at another because of some real or fancied slight. Sometimes, also, the difference may have been due to the boy in whose company he happened to be. For one who was so excessivly self-absorbed, de Robespierre could be remarkably aware of his human environment: hence his oratorical successes in later life. He may have been merry with the gay, and solemn with the serious. He certainly was agreeable only to those whom he could bring himself to like.

At the end of his course of studies in the humanities, de Robespierre began to read law, which he could do without leaving his college. Once more he distinguished himself, and when he took his degree, in 1781, his merit was so outstanding that he was granted a gift of 600 livres, while his scholarship was transferred to his younger brother.

He returned to his native city, where he began to practise as a barrister. He set up house with his sister Charlotte. The other sister had died while he was at Louis-le-Grand. He took up his work with the devotion and seriousness that characterised him, and soon he found his services in great demand. He examined the causes he was expected to defend with scrupulous detachment, and more than once refused to take up a brief that was not to his liking. He also was inclined to give his assistance free of charge to those who otherwise would not have been able to afford it. Thus he rapidly acquired a reputation for painstaking honesty and philanthropy which was more flattering than remunerative, and it must have been a welcome event for his sister and himself when he was offered, in 1783, a place as judge in the episcopal court. This office did not preclude his continuing to practise at the bar.

The legal system at Arras was amazingly complicated; courts dating from the days when the city belonged to the Hapsburgs still competed with the royal and the episcopal jurisdictions. The bishop's court administered high and low justice within the precincts of the city, and not long after his appointment the young judge—he was then about twenty-five years of age—was placed in the invidious position of having to pronounce the death sentence upon a malefactor. That night, he was unable to sleep. He wondered whether a human being had the right to deprive another human being of his life. To soothe his qualms with the argument that if he had not pronounced the sentence someone else would have done it was not a way out for scrupulous de Robespierre. He possessed no grain of opportunism, and suffered from that kind of social conscience that makes a man feel personally responsible for all the evil he notices

14

about him. He decided henceforth never to take his seat in the episcopal court. This step did not affect his friendly relations with the Bishop of Arras, who was by way of being a protector of his family, and he continued, nominally, to be a judge till 1788.

Once more, Maître de Robespierre read briefs and appeared in court, and acted as a self-appointed counsel for the poor. But others than the needy and the defenceless began to learn the way to his chambers. There was, for instance, the affair of the lightning conductor. In 1784 he appealed on behalf of M. de Vissery de Bois-Valé against a decision of the aldermen of Saint-Omer, who had ordered the removal of a lightning conductor from the appellant's house because they believed that it would endanger his neighbours. Maximilien spoke as an apostle of enlightenment and science, referred to Benjamin Franklin and the emancipation of the human mind, and his triumph was celebrated in the local papers and became the talk of all northwestern France.

If success be the reward of application, de Robespierre amply deserved to succeed. His life was a model of single-minded devotion to duty. He rose about six, worked till eight, when the barber came to shave him and powder his hair. The care he took of his appearance has become proverbial. He spent most of the day in court, and in the late afternoon he went for a solitary and meditative walk—a practice which Jean-Jacques Rousseau had made fashionable. The evenings were spent in reading and work. Occasionally the afternoon walk was varied by a visit to a friend, sometimes friends called at the home of Charlotte and Maximilien.

Maître de Robespierre was frugal. He was indifferent to the fare his sister provided, so long as it contained fruit, of which he was fond and consumed large quantities to correct a costive tendency. He was especially partial to oranges. He drank water slightly tinted with wine, but he did enjoy his cup of black coffee after lunch.

It did not take long for his fellow-citizens to discern his merit. Maximilien was not a prophet without honour in his country. Like many other provincial towns, Arras boasted its local academy, a literary and debating society modelled upon the French Academy of Paris. To it all that was socially noteworthy belonged, somewhat irrespective of knowledge or of talent. These academies exercised a considerable influence upon contemporary thought mainly through the competitions they frequently organised. It was in connection with such a competition that Rousseau for the first time sharply formulated his social doctrines. A similar competition caused de Robespierre himself, as we shall see, to launch into publication. Even before fame had touched him as a result of the affair of the lightning conductor he was elected a member of the Academy of Arras, in November 1783, and five months later he was received into the bosom of this distinguished company. He soon became its secretary, and before long its chairman. Here as elsewhere he imposed himself upon the attention of his fellow-men by personality and single-minded devotion.

So far, we have drawn but one side of the picture. Those staggering traits of absentmindedness, one or two of which Charlotte de Robespierre reports in her memoirs, were not solely the result of Maximilien's absorption in professional matters. He was a devotee of the doctrines of social and moral reform that were current in his day. These theories coloured his activities as a lawyer, they were the companions of his lonely walks, and when he sat up far into the night it was in order to read and to meditate more often than to prepare his pleadings.

In the 1780's whoever read and thought in France was 'enlightened.' Enlightenment was not a new movement that had suddenly taken hold of the minds of men. Ever since the Renaissance had widened the intellectual horizon of the élite, and humanism had taught them to look upon human beings as the aim and purpose of all human endeavour, a continuous and distinguishable thread had run through the expressions of systematic thought. The Reformation brought heaven within the reach of individual men and liberated them, in theory at any rate, from their dependence upon patented middlemen. Revelation in the shape of a book, somewhat obscure perhaps, and often hardly relevant, but written in the vulgar tongue, became available to all. And while the establishment of absolute monarchies appeared at first sight a retrogression from the political freedom and individualism of the Middle Ages, it was in reality part of the process by which the young nations were outgrowing the guardianship of the papacy. In the seven-

teenth century men made great strides towards
the rational explanation of nature that brought
it within the scope of humanism. Slowly emancipation spread to other planes. On the
threshold of the eighteenth century Locke had
proclaimed the doctrine of popular sovereignty,
which regarded the state not as the master of
men, but as a machine functioning for their
benefit. Men the centre of the universe, the
universe ruled by reason—this was the basic
doctrine of the new Renaissance. In many
countries enlightened despotism endeavoured
to govern in accordance with these doctrines.
France alone stuck to the practice and even to
the theory of absolute rule, which had long
since fulfilled its historic function.

Yet France was the centre of enlightenment.
From her radiated, in formulations that grew
in lucidity and cogency, the doctrines of freedom and popular sovereignty generated by
Swiss, Dutch, and Anglo-Saxon brains. The
system of Rome, refuge of darkness and con-
servatism, wilted away in the brains of thinking
men under Voltaire's acid sarcasm. Montesquieu popularised the English conception of
parliamentary government and of the right of
citizens to the protection of the Law, which is

supreme in the state. Rousseau justified his awkward behaviour in elegant drawing-rooms by pouring scorn upon convention, and palliated his sense of inferiority by praising to the sky the principle of popular sovereignty by which his Genevese fatherland ruled itself.

Prelates and noblemen, lawyers and officials absorbed the new principles and talked of freedom and equality. Neo-classicism gave rise to a fresh admiration for the virtues of Spartan, Athenian, and Roman republicanism. Every intellectual became a republican without ceasing to be a royalist. France, absurdly divided by feudal and local custom, had to be unified if she was ever to become rational. To achieve unity without a king appeared impossible. All this mental activity, this ceaseless probing into the outworn absurdity of institutions, this building of utopias and of a new body of political doctrine was in fact, though men did not know it, the intellectual preparation of the French Revolution. The existence of a body of revolutionary doctrine does not by itself mean revolution. There is no revolution without the existence of social and economic conditions that clamour for redress or readjustment. But such conditions by themselves are also incapable of producing revolution. Revolutions are the issue of the marriage of doctrine and economic conditions.

Maximilien became acquainted with the *philosophes* while he was still a pupil of the Collège Louis-le-Grand. He read Voltaire and Rousseau. From Voltaire, no doubt, he imbibed the humanitarianism and the burning hatred of injustice and oppression. He became converted to the master's deism. But the scepticism and irony of Voltaire's works he failed to perceive. To subtlety he was by nature blind. He never accepted the whole of Voltaire, and at a period when this author was still believed to have earned immortality by his tragedies, Maximilien saw already that his real merit was to be sought in his other writings. Rousseau was much more to de Robespierre's taste. The frenzied and cock-sure Genevese provided his literal-minded reader with guidance and doctrine for the rest of his life.

During his leisure hours the young barrister re-read Rousseau and studied Montesquieu, Beccaria, and other writers. There were good booksellers at Arras, and friends who were as willing to lend as to borrow books. And presently, the desire arose in him to contribute himself to the output of reformist literature. The occasion was furnished by the Academy of Metz, which, in 1783, had offered a prize for the best essay in answer to the question: 'What is the origin of the opinion which extends to all the members of the family of a guilty person a portion of the infamy attached to the opprobrious penalties imposed upon the culprit? Does this opinion cause more harm than good? If this question is answered in the affirmative, what are the remedies that could be applied to this state of affairs?'

A first batch of replies failed to satisfy the academicians. Once more, in 1784, they set the question, and Maximilien decided to compete. His legal studies and three years of legal experience as well as his copious reading made his task an easy one. But competition was keen, and the prize was allotted to a Paris lawyer, whose style was certainly more elegant than that of Maximilien. Maximilien, however, was given a second prize of equal value to the first. He published his essay at once, and also made it the basis of his inaugural address to the Academy of Arras.

There is a striking resemblance between the two essays, which proves to what extent ideas of social and legal reform were common property at the period. Of the two successful competitors de Robespierre expressed himself with more determination. The comparison shows how, when he was twenty-six, his convictions were what they remained throughout, free of compromise, based upon abstract principles, completely unoriginal. Most of his later opinions, all the principles that guided his actions in years to come, are contained in this prize essay. He naturally condemned the opinion to which the Academy of Metz had referred, and, in so doing, he managed to express his faith in the enlightenment of his century. 'In an enlightened age,' he wrote, 'when all things are weighed, judged and discussed, when the voice of humanity resounds with so great a strength, when our sensitiveness and delicacy have been enhanced by the progress of our knowledge, we incessantly endeavour to diminish the number of our ills and to increase the good things we can enjoy. In such an age an atrocious custom cannot hold out much longer.' This was progress, and progress by reason. All that was wrong was bound to be swept away by knowledge, because knowledge made men better, *plus sensibles et plus délicats.* The author knew the standard of social utility, the measure by which men could determine whether a thing would be beneficial or harmful. This measure was justice. 'Nothing is useful that is not just, and virtue produces happiness as the sun produces light.'

According to de Robespierre the source of the evil referred to in the question propounded by the Academy of Metz was inequality. When the misdeeds of nobleman and commoner are punished in the same way penalties will cease to be infamous or honourable, crime itself will be the only infamy. This equality of punishment will come when all individuals are members of the state in their own right; then the actions of other individuals will no longer affect them. This, of course, is the doctrine of popular sovereignty, the highest form of which, according to de Robespierre, was to be found under a republican system of government. But, like that of his fellow-reformers, his republicanism was an abstraction. It did not prevent his praising Louis XVI, upon whom many men still looked as a reformer. His egalitarianism of course also made him an anti-feudalist, but not a collectivist.

Stimulated by his success, de Robespierre

decided to compete for another prize, offered by the Academy of Amiens for the best essay in praise of the poet Gresset. The prize was not awarded to his essay, and he published it at his own expense in 1785. Gresset (1709-77) was a native of Amiens, and the author of slight, fugitive poems, of an epic dealing with the adventures of a parrot, and of a drama. An essay in his praise appears at first sight to call for qualities very different from those that brought success in a sociological essay. But it was with the same pen that de Robespierre traced his *Eloge*. In overpraising the literary merits of Gresset he showed himself to be a child of his time. Criticism, however, was not his main concern. He celebrated Gresset as a just and virtuous man, and delivered himself of a sermon on the moral and social bases of virtue. It is interesting to observe how deeply convinced he was that moral wickedness has its root in social injustice. The enormous demand for new luxuries had, in his opinion, destroyed the barriers that held evil passions in check, and had allowed them to overflow and damage the human landscape. Paris in particular was badly affected, 'Paris, that immense city whose conduct accustoms our eyes to the spectacle of every excess,' as the young prophet exclaimed.

A remedy to all these evils was not indicated in the *Eloge de Gresset,* unless it consisted in the imitation of Gresset's virtue, morality and love of religion. Perhaps the subject did not call for a concrete system of moral improvement. Perhaps, also, our author found it more congenial already to deal with general principles rather than to cope with their particular application.

We should, also, not fail to note the fact that 'the Roman' pronounced himself against a dictatorship. Once we find it possible to believe in his good faith—a conclusion not difficult to draw from the study of his life— we shall find such a pronouncement important, because de Robespierre never reached an opinion lightly, and because he never forgot. Gresset, then, was praised by him for having refused to become perpetual president of the Academy of Amiens. 'He deemed a dictatorship to be incompatible with the constitution of a literary republic, and he would have scrupled to accept a title of pre-eminence over those whose equal he was proud to be.'

It is, indeed, not surprising that de Robespierre's fellow-citizens looked upon him as a somewhat solemn personage. He had achieved a certain reputation that had spread beyond his native town. He was known as a reformer, and rather austere. He had tired people, upon occasion, with those words of 'freedom,' 'equality,' 'justice,' and 'virtue' that seemed ever to crop up in his conversation. Women gave him the respectful admiration they are so ready to lavish upon the successful, and liked, or pretended they liked, to read the speeches he had made at the bar. He would sometimes send the text of one of his speeches to a lady, and accompany it with a letter couched in the terms of factitious courtesy characteristic of the epoch. But few people realised to what extent earnest Maximilien could unbend when he wished. During a stay with some relatives at Carvin he sent a letter to a friend describing the journey and singing the praises of Carvin pastry.

'Every moment since our arrival has been devoted to pleasure,' he wrote. 'Ever since last Saturday I have eaten tart without heeding the envious. Fate has ruled that my bed should be placed in the room where the pastries are kept. What a temptation to spend the night eating up the store! But I reflected upon the beauty of mastering one's passions, and I went to sleep in the midst of all these seductive objects. It is true that during the day I made up for this long deprivation.' Then he produced a little poem of his own in praise of the art of the pastry-cook, and proceeded: 'Of all the traits of ingratitude of which mankind has been guilty towards its benefactors, none has revolted me more than the way it has forgotten the first maker of pastries. It is incumbent upon the people of Artois to atone for this crime, since in the eyes of Europe they are the best judges of tart. This glorious distinction imposes upon them the duty of erecting a temple to the inventor of pastry. Let me confess to you that I have a plan in this matter which I intend to put before the Estates of Artois. I count upon its receiving the powerful support of the members of the clergy.'

Maybe it is the playfulness of an elephant strumming upon the piano. But if the fun is clumsy, it is intended as fun, nevertheless. Maximilien de Robespierre wanted to smile and to raise a smile.

A few years passed, and the gentlemen of Arras realised that the young lawyer's lips were not always pursed, that his brow was not always wrapped in a cloud. In 1787 they invited him to join the brotherhood of the Rosatis. Secret societies were the fashion. Freemasons, Rosicrucians, and others forgathered with solemn ritual to discuss the final enlightenment of the world and to foster brotherhood by means of banquets. To these serious bodies the Society of Rosatis stood in about the same relation as the *Magic Flute:* it was an amiable game. It had been founded in 1778, and consisted of lawyers, officers, priests and noblemen, pretty much the same people who formed the Academy of Arras. One of these members was the lawyer Leducq, who possessed a valuable collection of Flemish primitives, and some pictures by Teniers and Van Dyck. Once a year, in June, they walked to a rose garden by the river Scarpe, where they celebrated the initiation of new brethren. Each candidate had to pick a rose, inhale its perfume three times, and fix it in his buttonhole. Then he had to drain a glass of *vin rosé* at one draught to the health of all Rosatis past, present and future, and kiss a member 'of whom he was fond' in the name of the whole society. He was then initiated into the secret doctrine, which was conveyed to him

29

in a speech delivered by an initiate. The new brother was informed of the fact that the society had existed as long as there had been roses and men of genius, and that Socrates, Euripides, Demosthenes, Horace, Virgil, Charlemagne and Henri IV, to mention but a few, had belonged to the society and were still alive, because no Rosati could die as long as he loved the rose and loved his brethren. Finally, amidst more drinking, the new member was made to sing an impromptu song in order to prove that he had duly received and understood the esoteric doctrine.

Maximilien bravely went through the ceremony of initiation, though he found it difficult to live up to what was expected of him. He was gently chaffed because he failed to drink as copiously as Leducq, the owner of the pictures. One of the brethren accused him of drinking nothing but water.

> Est-il aiguière,
> Serait il aqueduc?
> Ah, cher Robespierre,
> Imite donc Leducq,

he sang, and all the brethren took up the chorus. It would appear that the neophyte had hopes of turning the society into something more serious than it had been hitherto. In the speech of welcome he had to make at the reception of another member he declared that the new brother had been elected because he had always shown himself humane, full of sentiment, and just. Whether under his influence or not, the Rosatis began to discuss the philosophers, especially Rousseau, without, however, abandoning their more congenial pastimes of poetry-reading, singing and drinking.

However, de Robespierre did his duty. On the day of initiation he sang his own song, and he sang it very flat. There was little music in his soul. He subsequently wrote some poems in the manner of the Rosatis, which was the manner of the period, and recited them at various meetings of the society. One only among these poems deserves to be remembered. It is the madrigal to Ophelia, precise, formal, and mechanical. It dates as much as an epigram of Oscar Wilde. And yet, it has the charm of a faded piece of paper, brown along the creases, covered in an old-fashioned, feminine hand, and still faintly scented with musk, the charm of a worn-out, tinkling musical box that plays one single tune:

Crois-moi, jeune et belle Ophélie,
Quoiqu'en dise le monde et malgré ton miroir,
Contente d'être belle et de n'en rien savoir,
Garde toujours ta modestie.
Sur le pouvoir de tes appas
Demeure toujours alarmée.
Tu n'en seras que mieux aimée
Si tu crains de ne l'être pas.

Recipients of a little poem or a smart epistle, Ophelia and other women came and went, the objects of a short-lived amorous badinage. Maximilien's sister asserts that upon one woman, with the Rousseau-esque name of Anaïs Deshorties, his fancy rested a little longer. Perhaps a promise of marriage was exchanged. We do not know. But when Maximilien left Arras, Annaïs soon consoled herself and found a husband.

Serious work and solemn play were enough for the virtuous man. In his life, there was no room for women.

III

THE DEPUTY

THE old régime was disintegrating.

The educated had lost faith in it: they were rationalists and saw that it was absurd. Some who did well under it, the highest nobility, the princes, wanted it to last, even though absurd. But they saw that the King, chivalrous, empty-headed, weak and narrow-minded, would not serve as a prop for the system. And so they intrigued, with the King, about the King, against him, and worked, unwittingly, for the downfall of the old order. The nobility was torn by jealousy; so was the clergy, with its highly endowed, often unbelieving prelates and its hard-working underpaid parish-priests.

Then there was the unprivileged mass, a mass only to those who looked at it from the outside. Actually, the third estate was as much divided as the higher orders. There was a numerous lower middle class: shopkeepers and small peasants. And beneath the haves were the have-nots, the urban and the rural proletariat,

33

heavily taxed, ignorant, unvocal, capable of being swayed in any direction. But, economically on the level of the nobility, above it even, was the bourgeoisie. It had achieved economic power. Foreign trade, investment, speculation had brought wealth to the upper middle class. Industry too was playing an increasingly important part in the economic life of the nation. We have a tendency to imagine that the Continent waited till the beginning of the nineteenth century before it took its first hesitating step in the direction of industrialisation. As a matter of fact, metallurgy, shipbuilding, textile works were bringing prosperity to many, in France, before the advent of her political revolution.

The capitalist class, however, enjoyed neither political power nor social consideration. It was subjected to the innumerable pin-pricks of precedence and tradition. It was taxed unheard, and ruled unconsulted. One part of the bourgeoisie, indeed, had warred for generations against royal absolutism. The legal classes in their *parlements* (high courts of justice) had tried, but in vain, to impose their will upon the Crown. They were the focus of protest and discontent.

The old régime no longer corresponded to social realities. It was effete and creaking. Were an obstacle to arise, the impact would cause the machine to stop, perhaps to fall to pieces.

In the late 1780's everything went wrong at once. The King's government had engaged in a war to support the rebellious American colonies against England. It was a foolish war, inspired by pique, by old-fashioned royal pride with an admixture of the new semi-republican enlightenment. It drained the treasury, already badly depleted by the failure to distinguish between the public and the private expenditure of the Crown. The Queen and the favourites squandered millions in gambling, building, and feasting. From being a danger, state bankruptcy became a threat, almost a reality. The peasantry and the urban proletariat, more prosperous than those of other continental countries, were enlisted in the ranks of the discontented by a succession of industrial crises and bad harvests.

Without an aim, without a policy, the King and the Court fluttered from semi-enlightenment to despotism in the choice of ministers. The deficit grew. There seemed to be no way out: they appealed to the nation. The

Estates General, representative of the whole nation, must be called together. They must provide money, save the state, and disperse. They would make demands, perhaps. But the King would talk to them. He might even consent to a few reforms. No one, in this age of reason, was prepared to deny that there was an argument in favour of minor improvements. Indeed, quite a serious reform was granted very soon. The three orders, nobility, clergy and third estate, were convened, and the third estate was graciously permitted to send as many representatives as the two privileged orders together! But as the three would deliberate and vote separately, each order having one vote, there was little to fear from the one vote of the third, pitted against the two of nobility and clergy combined.

The Estates General were convened on August 8, 1788. It was a sensational event. Since the last Estates General had met, a period had elapsed as long as that which separates us from the coronation of King George III. France was electrified. Throughout the country, pamphlets were rushed through the press, discussing every aspect of the election. The King's subjects foregathered to decide what mandate they would give to their representatives. How were the elections to be organised? The government officials were not very certain, and did some hard work searching the archives.

The province of Artois was more familiar with election problems than many other parts of France, because it had Provincial Estates in which the three orders were represented. At this critical moment the rising barrister Maximilien de Robespierre felt it to be his duty to put at the disposal of his fellow-citizens the store of wisdom he had accumulated in the course of studies and meditation. He published an address to the people of Artois which proclaimed the prevalent doctrines of liberalism and reform. What distinguished his publication from many contemporary pamphlets was the emphasis he placed upon the humanitarian aspect of these doctrines, and his knack of following up every argument to its furthermost conclusion. He also displayed a Rousseau-like sensitiveness to human suffering. 'Our countryside offers the spectacle of unhappy people,' he wrote, 'who spray with tears of despair the soil their sweat has fertilised in vain! The major part of those who inhabit towns and country are lowered by want to that extreme degree of brutalisation in which man, entirely absorbed by the worrying necessity of preserving his existence, becomes incapable of reflecting upon the cause of his miseries and of recognising the rights he has been given by nature.' Already then Maximilien's penetrating eye had discovered the plotters, the vile ones, the cowardly, those who were deaf to the unuttered cry of the oppressed, those whose remedy differed from the remedy he proposed, the lukewarm, the uncertain. 'Vice, armed with unjust power, must itself learn to tremble before triumphant justice and reason!' Others wrote in the same vein. Maximilien meant every word he wrote. There lay the difference.

The members of the third estate in the Provincial Estates of Artois, argued de Robespierre, were not fairly chosen. In the name of the unrepresentative body atrocious injustices had been committed. Men were 'dragged into prison like criminals, beaten like slaves, for having dared to claim the sacred rights of property!' He invited his fellow-citizens to overthrow the Provincial Estates and to claim for themselves the right of appointing delegates to the Estates General.

The first issue of the address was soon exhausted. A second, enlarged edition appeared within a few weeks. The author had not put forward his own candidature, but he had made his mark: it would be impossible to overlook his claims. It was clear to him that no one discerned the truth as he did, that humanity, virtue, justice, freedom, equality, would never be served as they would be by himself. In March 1789 he went a step further and issued a second address describing the qualifications of the ideal delegate, an impressive human being indeed, honest, independent, firm, inspired by great conceptions. Clearly, the truest picture of the ideal delegate appeared in Maximilien's own looking-glass.

At this juncture he was called upon to act as counsel for a man who had been a victim of legal oppression. He had been kept in prison for years by means of one of those *lettres de cachet* which made it possible to deprive people of their freedom at the whim of an enemy or a disgruntled relative. In his address to the court he attacked the vices of the régime, and lectured the King about the political needs of the hour. After this the people of Artois could not fail to choose their reforming barrister.

The elections took place under what was

well-nigh universal suffrage. Maximilien was returned fifth on the list of the third estate of Artois. The stay at Versailles would be lengthy: all but the privileged wanted the Estates General to draw up a constitution for France. While the debates lasted, Maximilien would be entitled to a modest fee. So he gave up his practice, wound up his affairs, and started for Versailles. There he took lodgings at an inn with the other members for the third estate of Artois. He donned the sober black garb prescribed for those of his estate, and took part in the pageantry of the opening of the Estates General, on May 4, 1789. He listened to the early debates of the third, and began at once to form judgments upon his colleagues. The views expressed in letters to his friends at home breathe the doctrinaire enthusiasm, but also the suspiciousness that characterised him.

It cannot be said that the deputies were smaller than the events in which they took part. Though they did not foresee the vastness of the catastrophe that was going to engulf so many of them, they were to a surprising extent aware of the fact that they were making history. They knew themselves to be the mouthpiece of a nation that wanted to put an end to an absurd

and superannuated system of government.
They were used to the grandiloquent expression
of ample notions, they saw life through a series
of abstractions. They communed with the absolute. For most of them, it is true, the absolute
was somewhat divorced from reality. They
wanted freedom and equality in moderate doses.
Others wanted more: freedom and equality for
all, more than Rousseau's paradise on earth.
And they wanted it undiluted. Towards these
men Maximilien began to gravitate. He shed
the snobbish prefix *de* which placed him on the
fringe of the nobility and proclaimed the fact
that his ancestors possessed a coat of arms.

A first task found the third estate united.
They demanded the annulment of the measure
that prescribed separate voting by estate, with
its corollary, the drowning of the voice of the
third under those of the nobility and the clergy
combined. They resisted the Court, they proclaimed themselves a National Assembly, invited
the privileged orders to join them, and swore
an oath that they would not part before they
had given a constitution to the country. The
oath was such a fantastic departure from the
decorum and precedent of the old régime that
one deputy who had taken it went mad with

41

fear. The King changed his mind from day to day; the Paris mob, led by those who were soon to become the Jacobins and ultras, stormed the prison of the Bastille, the burghers banded themselves into a national guard, and the Court gave way. France had its Constituent Assembly. The King recognised the existence of a new sovereign, the French Nation.

In the course of these early debates Robespierre ascended the tribune on more than one occasion. The Assembly hardly listened: nobody knew his name. But he was persistent. He had a message to deliver, unambiguous but general, theoretic and urgent. He talked till he caught the eye of the leading men of the Assembly. Early in June he had become sufficiently known to be included in a deputation of twenty-four that was sent to the King. Events and his opinions were helping to put a mark upon Robespierre. For division was already ending the brief period of idyllic concord: the Assembly was beginning to separate into the haves and the friends of the have-nots. The moneyed bourgeoisie wanted to repress sedition as vigorously as it wanted to overthrow aristocratic privilege. Robespierre stood on the other side.

While still on the fringe of things, he already thought it necessary to divest himself of some of his natural sensitiveness. The poetic Rosati of Arras seemed to have been left centuries behind. He tried to justify the murder of a man by an infuriated mob. 'He has been executed by a decree of the people,' he wrote to a friend. But now, as before, he clung to his pathetic belief in the force of reason. 'Do you want the people to quieten down?' he exclaimed from the tribune. 'Speak to it in the language of justice and reason. Let it be certain that its enemies shall not escape the vengeance of the laws, and the sentiment of justice will succeed to that of hatred.' It sounded so clear, this muddle-headed doctrine of appeasement by the legal satisfaction of vindictive sentiments. He also urged that the new constitution should establish a court for punishing crimes against the nation. The idea was not his invention: Robespierre never invented. But from the beginning he recognised and adopted the notion of terrorism, without seeing as yet to what extremes faith and consistency would lead him.

Cowed by the epidemic of violence that suddenly swept over France, the Assembly, on the famous night of August 4, working itself into

43

a religious fervour of brotherhood—such were the times and such were the men—abolished all feudal privileges. But a few days later the temperature of the aristocrats and of the bourgeois who had bought feudal lands in recent years subsided. They were able to hedge the great sacrifice with so many concessions that little remained beyond an ineffectual proclamation of good intentions. Robespierre now sat with the ultra-democrats on the left of the chairman. Throughout this epic August he talked, often unheeded, once at least shouted down. In school-masterly fashion he lectured the Assembly on the imperfection of its rules of procedure. He quibbled about words, kept principles well to the fore, and supported the proposal for annual elections with arguments based upon the theory of popular sovereignty.

By the end of August the whole Assembly knew Robespierre. This he did not owe to his eloquence. His voice was not naturally agreeable. It was too thin, and he had a marked provincial accent. Nor was he a good improviser. He was at his best before a sympathetic audience, such as he found at a later period in the clubs to which he belonged, and when he had been able to write down, in his careful lawyer's hand, the points with which he intended to deal, and the figures and metaphors that were to illustrate them.

His appearance also was not calculated to arrest the attention. To us, the physical Robespierre looks more than a little blurred. The impressions he left upon his contemporaries were curiously contradictory. In the process of transmitting them to us they further allowed them to be modified by their prepossessions. The eyes left no vivid trace in men's memories. Robespierre was short-sighted, and the difficulty he found in focusing objects through his thick glasses gave him an appearance of shiftiness and of inability to look people in the face. The virtue of a straight gaze is often overrated. The more charged with thought and personality a man happens to be, the more difficult he may find it to gaze into the eye of the man he addresses. Robespierre was pregnant with notions: he looked over people's shoulders rather than in their eyes. And so men forgot his eyes, or remembered only that they were vaguely green and in no way memorable. We know that he was short, hardly more than five foot three, and slender.

Upon the contradictory testimonies and not

easily reconcilable likenesses we possess, M.
Mathiez, who revolutionised the historiography
of the French Revolution and was the champion
of Robespierre worship till his death in 1932,
found it possible to base a pen sketch that is
more valuable by its precision than by its
historicity. At the age of twenty-five, according to M. Mathiez, Robespierre was 'slender
and distinguished looking, with a broad fore-
head under a carefully groomed wig, light and
gentle eyes' (has a short-sighted person ever
possessed harsh eyes?), 'definitely arched eye-
brows, a delicate mouth under a long nose of
which the tip was upturned, round cheeks, a
rather strong chin.' His appearance, in any
case, mattered little: Robespierre was an
abstraction. Tangible and memorable were
his tidiness and the care he took of his person.
When he cast off the black uniform of a delegate of the third estate, he resumed his usual
garb: a green coat, a coloured waistcoat—
often made of satin and embroidered with pink
silk, dark breeches, and boots that covered the
calf.

A snub by the Assembly or by its chairman
that prevented his delivering a speech against
the proposal to give the King the right of

vetoing legislation provided the occasion that made Robespierre known to the people of Paris. He expanded the notes he had prepared and published the speech. It was read with approval. For Paris felt very strongly on the matter of the veto. When, on October 5, the Paris mob, infuriated by the shortage of bread, marched to Versailles and forced King and Assembly to return with it, Robespierre had ceased to be obscure. He was a popular man.

IV

THE JACOBIN

THE sovereign Constituent Assembly continued to meet in Paris until its dissolution in September 1791. It gave France a constitution based upon the principles of philosophy, as decentralised as the administration of the absolute monarchy had been centralised. Inspired less by anti-clericalism than by sheer financial necessity, it nationalised the properties of the clergy. It authorised the issue of paper money for which these properties were expected to provide a cover. Considered from the point of view of the old régime, the work of the Constituent Assembly was revolutionary enough. The Court submitted from necessity only, the King and especially the Queen did all they could secretly to enlist the support of foreign Powers against the representatives of the nation. But for all the hatred it aroused among the supporters of the old dispensation, the Assembly was revolutionary in a limited sense only. As Aulard puts it, 1791 was the year in

48

which the bourgeoisie took possession of the City. Though it hated aristocratic intrigue, though it welcomed, as on the famous fifth of October 1789, the intervention of the mob that supported the new régime against military coercion, yet it feared the proletariat even more than the enemies from above. It divided the nation into active and passive citizens, and though equality had been proclaimed as one of the rights of man, the vote was given only to those who paid the equivalent of three days' wages in direct taxation, while none who paid less than a silver marc (about fifty francs) could be elected as a representative of the people.

Against these distinctions the radicals in the Assembly ceaselessly protested, though usually without avail. Earnest enough in its defence of the Revolution, the bourgeoisie was determined that the Revolution should remain its own preserve, liberal, moderate, undemocratic. Weak and often uncertain of a hearing in the Assembly, the radicals enjoyed growing support in the country. This support was of two kinds. Where economic necessity drove men to violent action, action was often spontaneous. But in many cases conscious guidance was given to

49

democratic movements by middle-class in-
tellectuals. The decentralisation imposed upon
France by the theorists of the Assembly was
undone by enthusiasm fostered in Paris. Con-
federation united what the constitution had
divided, and France was beginning to speak a
language that differed from that of the majority
of its representatives.

To all outward appearance the dominant
figure in public life was Lafayette. Vain,
picturesque, surrounded by a halo of glory
acquired during the American Revolution, the
nobleman on his white horse basked in popular
ovations, organised the middle-class national
guards, dreamed of royalist constitutional
utopias inspired by Montesquieu, England and
Washington, and was the devoted servant of
the liberal moderates. The Assembly itself was
ruled by another nobleman, Mirabeau, eloquent, dissolute, corrupt, and yet a genuine
idealist. His revolution was more restricted
even than that for which the liberals were
working. He received a secret subsidy from
the Court, was friendly with all parties, and
with his thundering voice managed to shout
himself into a popularity that extended far
beyond the precincts of the Assembly. He was

the antithesis of Robespierre and his single-track mind. Robespierre, who wavered between distrust and admiration in his attitude towards Mirabeau, never felt completely easy about him.

At the Assembly in Paris Robespierre was what he had begun to be at Versailles. No longer unknown, he grew remarkably unpopular with the majority of his colleagues. Their hatred, reflected in the increasing violence with which royalist and bourgeois newspapers singled him out for attack, increased as his radicalism became more manifest. He missed no opportunity to bear witness to the truths that had been revealed to him. He spoke in and out of season, improving in technique as time went on, often shouted down or listened to with impatience, almost never able to carry the meeting with him. Every incident provided an opening for a declaration of principles, every problem was treated by him from the point of view of the absolute with which he communed. He never swerved from the straight course. He never felt the need of advice. Not that he was closed to outside influence. Unpractical, unable to deal with the concrete and the particular, he was easily influenced in matters of policy. Towards novelties he adopted precisely the same attitude as towards the abuses he had combated: he merely asked himself whether they were in agreement with the Doctrine.

The Doctrine, indeed, was simple enough. Reason taught that all men were born equal and free. The lack of virtue of certain men—rulers, aristocrats, pleasure-seekers—had caused the obscuring of reason and the consequent decay of equality and freedom. Awaken reason, restore virtue, and equality and freedom would return. The process of restoration might have to be violent, the suppression of moral evil ruthless. Freedom might have to be suspended in the process—but equality never.

Into minds that dwell in the absolute the notion of an interregnum of relativity enters with surprising facility. We notice the same capacity in most of the totalitarians by whom we are surrounded nowadays. The communist considers himself a democrat at heart, and is prepared to allow democratic methods on the very day democracy unreservedly adopts his economic philosophy. Fascists believe in the advent of an Italy free from delation and *confino,* Nazis in a fatherland where all will be nordic and servile without the threat of torture. Robespierre, who thirsted for the reign of meekness and reason, gradually found himself forced to admit that for the very sake of their existence the practice of these virtues had to be postponed for the time being.

It was reluctantly and after a long struggle that Robespierre adopted the view that freedom might have to be suspended for a while, until the Revolution had run its course. Especially in the early days he frequently stood before the Assembly as the defender of freedom. He opposed martial law, the decrease of the pensions of ecclesiastics, inquisitorial methods of income-tax collection, the establishment of a government monopoly for tobacco, and even the violation of the secrecy of letters and legislation to curb emigration. The last two measures were supported by all the radicals, but in the service of freedom Robespierre did not fear to court unpopularity even among the unpopular. He never was a politician or a time-server.

Equality was championed by Robespierre in the Constituent Assembly with greater fervour and still more conviction. Here no temporary suspension appeared conceivable. He pleaded for the political emancipation of Protestants and Jews, for the equal treatment of naval ratings and officers—much to the disgust of liberal bourgeois and aristocratic sympathisers —and for the equal right of all children to inherit their parents' property. He opposed the exclusion of the poor from the national guard. He was most insistent in his opposition to the measure by which the vote was withheld from the poor and only the well-to-do declared eligible to the legislature. In this matter, for once, his agitation was not barren of all results. In January 1790 he was able to demonstrate that the electoral system would disfranchise the province of Artois because there direct taxation was unknown. In consequence of his speech it was decided to suspend the principle of the silver marc in territories that had no direct taxation, until the system was made uniform for the whole of France. His local opponents tried to persuade the people of Artois that Robespierre's purpose had been to cause their taxes to be raised. Even in the first rounds his opponents were not above using unfair weapons.

Far from wishing to increase the burdens of the poor, Robespierre was ever at work to improve their condition. His attitude in economic matters was that of a typical radical of our day. 'Legislators,' he exclaimed in April 1791, 'you will have done nothing for freedom unless your laws tend by gentle and efficacious means to diminish the extreme inequality of fortunes!' This and many similar utterances reveal him not only as one who accepted the existence of property, but as a moderate, as one who might nowadays be called a revisionist or a gradualist. He certainly disliked property. On one occasion he called it 'a necessary and incurable evil.' But he was not a collectivist.

In those days Robespierre had hardly any private life. For a while, after he arrived in Paris, he is said to have had a mistress to whom he paid what might be called a retaining fee. But more and more his work monopolised him. To his work he gave all his energy, almost the whole of his time. He shared a small lodging with an acquaintance, but the two saw little of each other. Robespierre was hardly ever at home. The Constituent Assembly, however, received but part of his enthusiastic labours. Faithful though he was in performing his duties as a representative of the nation, it was in the political clubs that were springing up everywhere that his main interests lay. There he found an atmosphere more congenial than in the Assembly, and that unanimity of inspiration, if not of principles, so essential to the successful unfolding of his oratory.

There were, first of all, the *grands clubs*. Their origin was matter-of-fact, almost modest. At Versailles the deputies had formed the habit of meeting in small caucuses to discuss the attitude they would take in the Assembly. Some Brittany radicals had founded the Club Breton, to which Robespierre was soon admitted. The club flourished. When the Assembly moved to Paris it took over the premises of the Black Friars, popularly known as the Jacobins. As a result the club itself became known by that name. Its official title was 'The Society of the Friends of the Constitution.' Non-parliamentarians were admitted. Other societies outside Paris sought affiliation to it, and soon its ramifications covered the whole country. The subscription was substantial, the membership entirely bourgeois. The Jacobins' task was mainly to keep alive and develop the theory of the Revolution. They became the soul of the revolutionary movement, they developed a ritual, launched slogans, and wore badges and distinctive signs. They possessed all the characteristics of the cells and organisations from which the totalitarian administrations of to-day draw their main strength: fervour, intolerance, an inclination to violence, a vast capacity for hero-worship, and a prudent readiness on the part of moderates to allow extremer members to set the tone at their meetings.

The Jacobins, though bourgeois, turned more towards radicalism as time went on. They were impatient of the liberals' efforts to restrict equality to those above the proletariat. Only the Marxist to whom faith has been given can discover the economic mainspring of Jacobinism. The undogmatic student of history must turn to psychology in order to understand how the Jacobins could act in direct opposition to their class interest. The Jacobin must remain an enigma to us unless we realise that his frame of mind was unusual. He was rational but unreasonable, unselfish, fervently emotional, unable to respond to the stimuli that affect human behaviour at ordinary times, unable to respond to them, at any rate, in a normal fashion. He was the victim of the

57

most intense form of suggestion. There is latent in all of us an impulse towards subservience, an impulse which is but one manifestation of that surplus vigour we are unable to spend upon the business of preserving and transmitting our existence. Sometimes a forceful personality, an ideal, a slogan, arouses in us this impulse of subservience and makes it a motive of unselfish activity. The moral qualities of the personality, the intrinsic value of the ideal or the slogan are immaterial. Nor is it necessary that there should be deliberate intent on the part of any one to arouse the impulse. Circumstances, the fact that men are gathered together in crowds, the pomp of religious or state ceremony, the rhythmic noises that accompany martial display, can achieve the same result. There are also periods in history when a tense, collective expectation of strange or better things to come increases general suggestibility. Communism, fascism, naziism, revivalism, the Oxford movement, the royal jubilee, and the efficacy of recruiting bands in times of war all belong to this category of psychological phenomena. Here, and here alone, lies the explanation of Jacobinism. Here, also, that of the mentality of Robespierre.

By the side of the *grands clubs* of the bourgeoisie other clubs sprang up in popular quarters. In the summer of 1790 was formed the 'Society of the Rights of Man,' called the club of the Cordeliers (Grey Friars). The origin of this name is similar to that of the Jacobins. The Cordeliers were less concerned with theory: while they aimed at educating the masses in revolutionary doctrine, their main purpose was to compel those in power to observe the general principles of freedom and equality. They denounced all offences against these principles before the tribunal of public opinion. They charged a low subscription, no one was precluded from joining them. They grouped around them other societies, composed exclusively of poor people.

Both among the Jacobins and the Cordeliers, though he did not actually join the latter, Robespierre rose rapidly in importance. In April 1790 he was elected to serve a period as president of the Jacobins. A year later, when Mirabeau died, he became the undisputed favourite of the popular societies. At the Cordeliers, his speech in favour of universal suffrage, which he had been unable to deliver to the Assembly and had therefore published in pamphlet form, was read from the tribune, republished at the expense of the society, and posted up all over the country. Affiliated societies were invited to acquaint themselves with the opinions of 'a soul that was just and pure,' heads of families were recommended to teach its principles to their wives and children. Henceforth, Robespierre was the leader of the radicals. His portrait was to be seen in the windows of all the print-sellers. At the Salon of 1791 two pictures of him were exhibited, and underneath one of them was written the name by which people were beginning to call him: the Incorruptible.

It was at this period also that the Assembly, impressed by the power of the politically conscious citizens he now represented, listened to him and followed his advice on two important matters. First he made the Assembly decide that none of its members could be appointed to any official post, then he persuaded it to decree that none of its members should be eligible for the next Legislative Assembly. There was no question of tactics in this. Robespierre disqualified himself as well as his colleagues. He was animated by considerations of political purity, and he carried the Assembly with him. The idealism of the early days was revived for one brief moment.

We shall have to deal sooner or later with this question of tactics and with Robespierre's alleged opportunism. There is no doubt that events helped Robespierre in his ascent to power in a way that might lead us to believe that all had been planned beforehand, were it not that at the end of the road stands the sharp silhouette of the scaffold to remind us, at the very least, that not everything had been planned. This place will serve as well as another to ask ourselves what we must think of the theory that Robespierre was a schemer. For in the self-denying decision of the Constituent Assembly, which was his work, can be seen the beginning of that impressive process by which his rivals were successively eliminated.

The coming Legislative Assembly, then, was to contain no member of the Constituent Assembly. This was but a small loss to the radicals. They were better organised than their opponents. Paris was becoming their own preserve. They could send their chosen spokesmen to the Legislative and keep an eye on them; the spokesmen would have behind them the whole fighting strength of the clubs. But the Legislative, purged of royalists, turned out in practice to be hardly less liberal-bourgeois than the Constituent Assembly, owing to the special outlook of a number of Jacobin new-comers. Then came the Convention—a new Constituent Assembly—and the committee system. Under this régime the liberal-bourgeois were decimated by the fall of the Girondins. Then, we are told, the semi-communist extremists were swept away with the aid of the moderate radicals, and finally Robespierre disposed of Danton and his fellow-radicals, who had no allies left. Henceforth, he was in power.

This analysis has the virtue, at any rate, of making supererogatory the formula of blood-thirstiness, sadism, and degeneration. But it is itself unsatisfactory. Was Machiavelli ever the slave of a theory? There is no need to endow Robespierre with fiendish foresight and calculation. Though human motives be complex and difficult to unravel, we are not justified in introducing out-of-the-way explanations unless the simpler and more obvious interpretations fail to apply. Now the complex and the subtle are entirely out of place in the case of Robespierre: his case is elementary: he was Mr. Everyman in the throes of a hundred per cent. certitude.

V

TRIBUNE OF THE PEOPLE

ROBESPIERRE was so certain about what he had decided to consider essentials that he could afford uncertainty about what seemed to him unessential. Like the English of to-day, most Frenchmen, in 1791, were royalist republicans. The word republic was used in a loose sense that did not necessarily pre-suppose the abolition of royalty, much as we speak nowadays of a British Commonwealth. There were some real republicans, but the liberals were royalist, and so were most of the radicals. Only a minority among the radicals wanted a change of régime. The nation was most emphatically loyal to its King. Louis XVI himself brought about a large-scale conversion to republicanism. On June 20, 1791, he fled with his Queen and his children, intending to return under the protection of anti-constitutional and foreign troops. He was stopped at Varennes and led back to Paris a prisoner.

At once republican propaganda flared up. Robespierre warned his followers against it. There was no difference in his opinion between a republic and a monarchy shorn of all its powers. Freedom, equality, and virtue could flourish under either. An oligarchic republic would be worse than a genuinely constitutional monarchy. Why, therefore, waste energy in demanding the abolition of an institution to which so many still attached value? He never wavered, however, in his determination to secure that the throne should be entirely subordinated to the will of the nation. The flight to Varennes offered an opportunity to press this point. The great majority of the Assembly were exercising their wits in order to save the King from the consequences of his action, and welcomed the fiction, more suited to the England of Gilbert and Sullivan than to the France of Rousseau, that the King had been kidnapped by enemies of the nation. Robespierre urged that the King and the Queen should be interrogated as to their share in planning the escape.

As yet the power of Robespierre over the Paris populace was far from absolute. He was unable to talk them out of their newly acquired republicanism. Petitions were organised requesting the Constituent Assembly to dethrone the King. Finally, a large-scale demonstration was organised by the left-wing radicals to be held on July 17 at the Champ de Mars, where a petition was to be signed. While the demonstration was in peaceful progress, Lafayette and his national guards appeared on the scene, fired at the crowd, and killed a number of them. The blood-bath had been organised beforehand. It was, as Aulard has written, 'a *coup d'état* of the bourgeoisie against the people, against all democrats, whether republican or not. It was an act of civil war, the beginning of the class-war.' For a moment violent reaction reigned. A number of radicals went into hiding. Their papers were searched by the police. Robespierre himself seems to have run some risk: the Cordeliers decided to provide him with an armed guard. In the end he was interrogated by the magistrates, but they declared him free from blame. We should remember how his liberal opponents were the first to resort to violence and repression, when we come to judge his actions later on.

There was now rising within Robespierre a strong feeling that the Revolution, his Revolution, was being sabotaged. The Constituent Assembly had resumed its old hostility towards him. Almost regularly it drowned his voice with the insistent and intolerant cry of 'aux voix! aux voix!'—the ' 'vide! 'vide!' of the House of Commons. So he decided to appeal to the country. In August he issued his *Appeal to the French*. In this significant utterance he warned the nation against those who tried by their manœuvres to guide the Revolution into a direction useful to themselves, in fact, towards the old despotism. These men would compel the people either to resume their chains, he wrote, or to buy freedom, so far conquered by the sole force of reason, at the price of blood. Robespierre, who only a few months earlier had made a fervent speech against the death penalty, which he called 'cowardly assassination' and 'a solemn crime,' was contemplating violence and bloodshed in defence of the Revolution. That dichotomy of which minds dwelling in the absolute are so unexpectedly capable was beginning to manifest itself in his case. Blood might have to be shed as the only method by which that state of freedom, equality, and virtue could be reached in which the death penalty would no longer find room.

In one of his last contributions to the debates of the Constituent Assembly Robespierre further elaborated the idea of special measures for the salvation of the Revolution. 'When I see on the one hand that the constitution, at the moment of its birth, is still surrounded by internal and external enemies,' he said, 'when I see that though speeches and appearances have changed while deeds remain what they were because only a miracle could have brought about a change of hearts; when I see intrigue and falsehood sound the alarm and at the same time sow trouble and discord; when I see the chiefs of warring factions fight less for the cause of Revolution than in order to seize power and dominate us in the name of the monarch;— when, on the other hand, I see the exaggerated zeal with which they prescribe blind obedience and proscribe even the name of freedom; when I see the extraordinary means they use in order to destroy the public spirit by the resurrection of prejudice, light-heartedness, idolatry;—then, indeed, I am unable to believe that the Revolution is over!' Sombre words in which is revealed a mind naturally gentle in the process of reconciling itself to the acceptance of violence.

The Legislative Assembly met on October 1, 1791, and Robespierre's mandate as a representative of the nation expired. He decided to devote himself to the defence of his principles by using the influence he had acquired in the clubs. But first he paid a brief visit to his native territory, where he was received with acclamation; at Arras the houses were illuminated, and a civic crown was offered to 'the defender of the people.'

There was indeed much work to be performed in Paris by a zealous watchdog of the rights of man. The Legislative contained more radicals than the Constituent Assembly, but they were still a minority. The majority was composed of sincere adherents of the constitution who were bourgeois and liberal, and no more friendly to absolute equality than their predecessors. But even the radicals contained a new element that soon enough provided the Incorruptible with reasons for apprehension. A solid phalanx of Jacobins had arrived in Paris from the south-western départements, as violent as any in their doctrine, yet, somehow, different from the purists who

69

had founded the Breton club. They became known by a geographical appellation: they were the Girondins, led by Brissot, Condorcet, Guadet, Roland. The Girondins have left a legend, or rather, the poet Lamartine wove a legend round their memory when he wrote their history in 1847. They were as romantic as he describes them, but less idealistic. Like nearly all Jacobins, they were bourgeois who had espoused the extreme popular cause against their own class interests. But some realisation of these interests, and to a greater extent their intellectual and artistic predilections, the fascination of salons and elegant company, in short, those subtle influences which advanced politicians of our own day call 'the aristocratic embrace,' had begun to temper the almost dionysiac frenzy of their earlier Jacobinism. The Girondins were ambitious. They wanted to create a new world-order, but they wanted to create it themselves. They desired immediate power. No longer able to spend itself upon agitation for total equality, their pent-up enthusiasm needed another outlet. This was provided by war, which is propaganda converted into action, accompanied by a nationalist fever closely akin to pure Jacobinism.

The Jacobins used to meet four times a week, in the evening, and at their meetings Robespierre was almost invariably present. After their day's work at the Legislative the Girondins also came, and it was upon this common ground that the first battles between them and Robespierre were fought. Robespierre often commented upon the work of the Legislative before his Jacobin friends. He invariably lifted the issue of the day into the realms of pure reason, from which humour was severely banished. He resented the tone of light-heartedness displayed by that old courtier, the minister Nabonne, used to the smooth superficialities of the old régime, when addressing the Assembly. 'Had I been in the chair,' declared Robespierre, 'I should have taken the liberty to remind this minister of the fact that he was in the presence of his superiors and judges, and that the tone that suits courtiers cannot be admitted in the sanctuary of the French senate.' Robespierre's debating manner was certainly different indeed. He once told the Jacobins how he would proceed himself: 'It is not by partial, incoherent measures, not even by flashes of wisdom and energy, that one leads a revolution to a success-

71

ful issue. A wisely combined system must be applied without intermission, by going back to the first causes of disorder, and by attacking them with sustained energy. It is in the light of these principles that I examine the questions that interest us.'

Such methods not seldom brought forth speeches that were dull beyond description, proceeding by deduction, subtle distinctions and contrasts. But they were listened to and appreciated because they dealt with matters that seemed vital to the audience. And there was something in the atmosphere also, the sombre oppressiveness of a gathering thunderstorm, that made men more sensitive, capable of being swayed by what soberer minds would have dismissed with a yawn. Moreover, Robespierre's utterances seldom lacked an element of sensationalism. He constantly warned the Jacobins about conspiracies that were afoot in the country. Lafayette was the special object of his distrust. His suspiciousness made him uncannily perspicacious, and subsequent revelations have proved how well-founded his allegations were.

It was mainly on the ground of his distrust of aristocratic conspirators and of the ill-will of the executive towards the Revolution that Robespierre opposed the war for which the Girondins were so persistently agitating in the Assembly and at the meetings of the Jacobins. For various reasons the nation, during the last months of 1791, wanted war. At one moment Robespierre stood entirely alone in opposing it. But being without ambition, he was never afraid to support an unpopular cause. Did he not, one day, make an impromptu speech against the wearing of the red phrygian cap which the Girondins were trying to introduce and to which the radicals had taken with their child-like zest for symbolism? On half a dozen occasions, in December and in January, he delivered brief speeches or lengthy addresses in which he coldly criticised the universal war-fever. He pointed out how dangerous war would be, how it would strengthen the hands of the monarchy and of the friends of the old régime, how it would lead to dictatorship and counter-revolution. His position was not that of an out-and-out pacifist. Certain forms of war he admitted. 'We must not wage the war of the Court nor of the intriguers the Court uses and who make use of it, but the war of the people,' he pronounced. 'The French people must rise and arm themselves integrally, either in order to fight a foreign foe or to thwart internal despotism.' In practice such an attitude hardly differed from a wholesale disapproval of any war that could be fought in existing circumstances. It was purely negative. But gradually the Jacobins who had chafed at first under his unemotional realism became converted, if not to the extent of accepting his views, at least to the point of listening to them with goodwill and of ordering them to be printed and distributed in the country.

He was defeated, of course, and war was declared against the Emperor on April 4, 1792. It was a triumph for the Girondins, but though Robespierre at once submitted to the decision of the majority and henceforth warmly supported all efforts to secure the effective waging of war, they could not forgive him for having stood in their way. A bitter feud broke out between Robespierre and the Girondins. These men, imbued with the spirit of the salons, had come to hate the pedant, and hated him all the more for being popular. There can be no doubt that they were responsible for introducing a personal animosity in what need only have been a difference of policy. They often tried to prevent Robespierre from obtaining a hearing at the club. Once, as he was alluding to the Supreme Being in the course of a speech, the Girondins, many of whom were unbelievers, created an uproar. He was abused with more virulence in their papers than he had been in the liberal journals that appeared under the régime of the Constituent Assembly. 'There are three views among the public on the subject of M. Robespierre,' said one of them. 'Some think he is mad, others ascribe his conduct to wounded vanity, and a third section believes that he is subsidised from the civil list.' When at last he retaliated in a speech and in the numbers of a review he was editing at that time, Robespierre was almost equally unfair. But he had one advantage over his opponents. Enamoured as they were of action and of power, they repeatedly showed themselves ready to compromise in order to achieve their immediate aim. They wavered and changed, and sometimes even attempted to reach an understanding with the Court. But the Incorruptible never altered.

More than once the quarrel was patched

up, and embraces, of which those sentimental readers of *La Nouvelle Héloïse* were so fond, took place in public to the plaudits of enraptured, moist-eyed Jacobins. But the two parties stood too close to one another, the differences in their principles were too small. They hated each other as only Protestants who have secured salvation by almost identical formulas, or members of two wings of an extremist political movement, can hate each other.

The war found the French army unequipped, unprepared. The Court communicated the plan of campaign to the enemy. Most generals and officers were disloyal, or rather, were loyal to the old régime. During April and June (1792) the soldiers ran away from the enemy and the French offensive was checked. Meanwhile a new economic crisis, due to the fall of the paper currency and intensified by speculation, caused a serious increase of radical agitation in the country and in Paris. Insurrection was in the air. We have already heard the hints Robespierre once dropped in justification of insurrection as the final resort of the oppressed. But it was not a method that appealed to him. 'It is a rare, uncertain, extreme method,' he said. When in June the Paris populace invaded the Tuileries—a premature and insufficiently prepared attempt to upset the throne—he expressed disapproval of their act because it was bound to strengthen the reactionaries. Indeed, it had almost the same aftermath as the republican petition movement in July of the previous year. Times had changed, however. War, with its inevitable appeal to general participation and the sacrifice of all, had emphasised the notion of popular sovereignty and brought a new awareness to the people. To this extent the predictions of the Girondins were fulfilled. But the movement went further. The provinces sent armed representatives to Paris, the so-called Fédérés, who greatly strengthened the power of popular resistance. On the road to Paris they had learned the battle hymn of the Marseilles contingent, and upon hearing the 'Marseillaise,' the most ego-obliterating war-song ever composed, Paris went mad. Robespierre himself experienced an elation which almost drove him into specific and concrete utterance. Welcoming the Fédérés at a meeting of the Jacobins, he said: 'Let us demand the faithful application of the laws, not of those that vouchsafe

77

protection to great criminals only, but of those that protect freedom and patriotism.' Here was a distinction. It grew more marked ere long: 'If you will not save the people,' he wrote in an address to the Legislative Assembly, 'tell them so, that they may work out their own salvation.'

The end of July was drawing near. Lafayette was threatening to play the part of Monk— three weeks later he surrendered to the enemy. 'Big evils call for big remedies,' said Robespierre at his club. 'The state must be saved. Nothing is unconstitutional except what ruins it.' He developed his plan in detail: a national convention was to be called together at once in order to democratise the constitution. It was to be elected by universal suffrage. Action to this effect was to be taken by the Legislative Assembly. And supposing the Assembly took no action? That contingency he left unmentioned. To be direct was not his way. He merely pointed to the alternative: the people could work out their own salvation!

There were others who saw to it that Robespierre's words should not remain a vain threat. While the Girondins were talking of arraigning him before the High Court, the committee of action which had recently been formed by the provincial Fédéré contingents that had remained in Paris was preparing a coup. It worked in close alliance with those Jacobins who had not come under Girondin influence and who were beginning to be known as the Mountain. Of the secret meetings they held Robespierre was informed: he took part in a few of them. But he had little share in the working out of the details of action. Intensive propaganda took place among the forty-eight sections of Paris, where for a long time citizens who possessed the franchise had been meeting daily. Latterly 'passive' citizens had been admitted to their meetings, while all but radicals were intimidated into staying away. During the night from August 9 to 10 the organisers of the coup warned the sections, who promptly sent their delegates to the Town Hall. There a revolutionary town council, the Paris Commune, was established. In the morning the Fédérés, led by the men of Marseilles, marched upon the Tuileries; the populace from the suburbs joined them, and the palace was stormed, not without considerable loss of life on both sides. The King took refuge with the Assembly, which suspended him from his office and handed him over for imprisonment and eventual trial to the revolutionary Commune.

This was the second French Revolution. Though he had neither led nor organised it, Robespierre had played a considerable part in preparing the atmosphere needed for its success. He was elected a member of the Commune, and repeatedly appeared as its spokesman at the bar of the Assembly. The Assembly appointed an executive council, a kind of ministry in which several Girondins and also the radical Danton were given a seat. Arrangements were made for reflecting a national convention by manhood suffrage, as demanded by Robespierre, and for six weeks Assembly and Commune shared power in France. It is during this period that further Austro-Prussian victories took place, and the horrible massacre of defenceless inmates of the Paris prisons. For these acts of rabble-terrorism Robespierre was not responsible. It is true that he took no steps to put an end to them. But his meditations on the subject, and his efforts to decide in the light of Rousseau and of absolute reason whether they were the rightful vengeance of that admirable and sinless entity, the people, or merely a vile orgy of bloodlust, were not terminated by the time the butchers' arms were stayed by physical exhaustion.

VI

A LITTLE BLOOD

THERE are two distinct periods in Robespierre's life. Till the fall of the Girondins in June 1793 —the event with which the present chapter will close—he was a critic, an agitator. Afterwards he wielded or shared power, or, if not power, responsibility. The stretch of nine months at which we have now arrived, from September 1792 to June 1793, forms a period of transition. It shows us Robespierre becoming familiarised with the idea that blood may be shed for lawful purposes, and accepting the view that, for the sake of democracy itself, democrats may, in exceptional circumstances, restrict its operation. But it also belongs to the previous period, because it witnesses the consummation of Robespierre's fight with the Gironde.

The Convention was elected by a minority: royalists and liberals were made to stay at home. But the radicals, for whose benefit the *journée* of August 10 had been organised, did

82

not dominate the Convention. They were not even masters of the Jacobins. Only at the Cordeliers and other popular societies did they reign undisputed, and there, indeed, extremism usually silenced all other forms of radicalism. Somewhat to his astonishment Robespierre, who had of course been returned to the Convention, discovered that there were by now revolutionaries more revolutionary than himself, purists of equality who wanted to go beyond his own radical utopia. The war had disorganised the production of goods and provisions, and paper money continued to decline in value. A wave of socialism passed over Paris. And so, while the fight against the Gironde, the dominant set in the Convention, went on, Robespierre and the other chiefs of the Mountain were compelled to cast anxious glances to the extreme left, to demand concessions for which these people pressed, and thus again to provide their chief opponents with arguments against themselves. The majority in the Convention wavered between Mountain and Gironde. It was called the Plain. The party that could acquire its support was almost sure of victory.

Socialist propaganda had frightened many

people. It produced an anti-socialist reaction in the Convention, which made it one of its first concerns solemnly to place property under the safeguard of the nation. This step met with Robespierre's approval. He was not a leveller. Did not Rousseau, the oracle, believe in private property? But Robespierre also believed in equality, and socialism was the logical conclusion of egalitarianism. There was thus an inherent contradiction between two of the main tenets of his creed, which he was never able to solve. At the same time the contradiction was not without its advantage. It enabled him to obey the dictates of circumstance, dictates that were not always consistent, without having to reproach himself with inconsistency. The socialist extremists played a considerable part in the shaping of events during the end of 1792 and the first months of 1793. We shall have more to say about them in a subsequent chapter.

The Girondins thought that they would throw discredit upon their hated opponent by accusing him of connivance with the extremists, by calling him a leveller. Simultaneously they accused him of aiming at a dictatorship, and they placarded these allegations all over Paris.

While immediately after the September massacres they had, like the other Jacobins, tried to pass over these awkward horrors in silence, they presently began to hint that Robespierre had organised them. Before the end of October the struggle between Girondins and Mountain had flared up hotter than before, and by singling out Robespierre among their opponents the Girondins contributed not a little to strengthen his position as a popular leader. Indeed, the Girondins were strangely unwise. They dreamed of power, and lacked political sense. In an age that was thirsting for theoretic certainty they remained obstinately empirical. 'Let us beware of metaphysical abstractions,' said Vergniaud. 'Nature has given passions to men, and it is through these passions that we must govern them in order to make them happy.' But the Girondins were less concerned with the passions of others than eager to satisfy their own. They played a reckless game and were short-sighted opportunists unaware of the danger of arousing suspicion, oblivious of the fact that they were living through a revolution, not moving in the artificial elegance of the old régime. They made an enemy of Danton, the unscrupulous and highly vulnerable but still

85

powerful Jacobin leader. They insisted upon his rendering accounts for the months when, after August 10, he had been Minister of Justice and virtual Premier of France. Poor Danton, who had squandered thousands and bought himself four or five properties in the country, was compelled to throw in his lot with the Mountain, though he would have preferred to work together with the adventurous and glamorous Girondins. His tempestuous eloquence, his gifts as a leader, were lost to them.

When the Girondins resumed their offensive, Robespierre retaliated, and struck out at his enemies with that self-righteous conviction which never deserted him. He accused them of having wished to raise the Duke of Brunswick, leader of the enemy armies, to the throne of France. The division continued to widen. Inevitably one side moved to the right, the other to the left. There were hardly any bourgeois liberals of the early-revolution type left in the Convention. The Girondins were driven by the force of events to take their place. All that was conservative, clerical, royalist even, rallied to their support. Thereupon those of their followers who were primarily Jacobins began to drift towards the Mountain, where their ideals were better understood. Thus another difference arose. Paris was radical and democratic. The administrations of the other départements, selected under the undemocratic franchise of the earlier days of the Revolution, were fairly conservative. As they moved towards the right, so the Girondins began to look with more favour towards them. They flattered the départements, put them in opposition against radical Paris. They pleaded for the right of France against Parisian oppression. They saw their own salvation in a decentralised administration, and some of them went so far as to suggest that départements should enjoy the autonomy of North American states. Thereupon their enemies accused them of being 'Federalists' and plotters against the unity of the Republic.

The Jacobins, before whom the battles of the Convention were fought afresh in the evening, sided with the Mountain. On October 10 they expelled Brissot from their ranks. A fortnight later they excluded a number of other Girondins. The Girondins were in a rage. Their speeches became more pointed. They no longer contented themselves with vague accusations. They appealed to the guillotine. On October 31, Isnard declared himself in favour of killing the enemies of freedom. About the middle of November he returned to the subject. He said that forgiving a crime amounted to sharing it, and that blood must be shed, if necessary. Gangrenous parts of the body-politic must be cut off. Again, at the end of the month, he exclaimed: 'By the word responsibility we mean death!' Other Girondins expressed their approval. Madame Roland, their elegant hostess and inspirer, wrote to her friends that freedom could be reached only through a sea of blood. The Girondins called up armed supporters from the provinces. It is true that soon enough Jacobin propaganda turned these new Fédérés into convinced supporters of the Mountain, but before their conversion they paraded the streets of Paris singing a song of which the refrain was a demand for the heads of Robespierre, Marat, Danton, and whoever dared defend them. A number of Robespierre's admirers feared that these threats might lead to an attempt against his life. Without his knowledge several of them constituted themselves into a bodyguard. A burly porter of the Halles appeared every morning outside his house, armed with a club, and followed him to the Convention, where he remained all day in the public gallery, never losing sight of him till he had seen him safely home. A printer's journeyman and a locksmith presently assisted him in carrying out his self-appointed duties.

The excesses of speech which the Girondins allowed themselves disgusted other people besides the Jacobins. The unattached members of the Convention, the so-called Plain, showed repeatedly that they objected to their tactics. When at the end of October a Girondin member, the novelist Louvet, delivered a great attack against Robespierre, once more accusing him of having openly aimed at dictatorship, the Convention decided to give the latter an opportunity of replying to his critics. Characteristically, Robespierre asked for time. His oratory had much improved by incessant practice. But except in a friendly atmosphere he was still a poor improviser. A week later he delivered his carefully studied reply. It was vigorous, it certainly proved that he had right on his side, in so far as right can ever be on one side. But even so he was rhetorical, artificial, fantastically syllogistic. Nevertheless, he carried the majority with him: the Convention and Paris considered that he had vindicated himself.

At this juncture the Mountain decided to press for the early judgment of the King who was still a prisoner at the Temple. They were actuated by considerations of party politics. They hoped that the debates upon the King's fate would take the people's mind off the social problems continually thrust into the foreground by extremist agitators. And they knew that they would create new difficulties for the Girondins who were still in power. The fact that their connections to the right were acquiring a considerable importance for them made the Girondins anxious not to be too hard on the King, while they also wished to give the country a share in deciding his fate, because this was another way of diminishing the importance of Paris.

For Robespierre the fate of the King presented a serious problem of conscience. He was still an opponent of the death penalty. But he was convinced that the present situation could not last without danger to the Revolution. Soon after the arrest of Louis XVI highly incriminating papers were found at the Tuileries. They proved what Robespierre had always suspected: the King was guilty of treasonable plotting with foreign and domestic enemies of the state. Robespierre was worried. What did his principles command? Clemency would be fatal. Anything short of the tyrant's death would leave him a potential rallying point for the enemies of freedom and equality. And yet all the arguments Robespierre had ever advanced against the death penalty applied to the case of Louis. He was saved from the cruel dilemma by the deputy Saint-Just. This young man, extraordinarily handsome with his blue, tender, penetrating eyes and his somewhat feminine face, had become a great friend of the Incorruptible. He had written to him, two years earlier, and told him of his admiration. Then, at the age of twenty-six, he arrived in Paris to become a member of the Convention, and placed his hard and sombre convictions and his great talents at the service of radicalism. Unlike his master, he was a man of action, capable of quick decisions.

No sooner was the question of Louis XVI raised than Saint-Just knew how to solve it. Justice, he stated, had nothing to do with it. The Revolution was fighting, the King was the enemy. Here, of course, was the formula

needed by Robespierre. There was no need
to give up his opposition to the death penalty.
To decree the death of Louis was not to execute
him: it was merely to extinguish the embodied
antithesis of the Revolution! On November
3, in the Convention, Robespierre took over
the thesis of Saint-Just. 'There is no question
of pronouncing sentence upon that man, but
of taking a measure of public safety,' he proclaimed. Indeed, if Louis could still be made
the object of a process, he might be acquitted;
he might be innocent. What do I say? He will
be presumed innocent until he is convicted.
But if Louis be acquitted, if he can be presumed
to be innocent, what becomes of the Revolution?' However, lest his conscience should fail
to be satisfied, Robespierre also paid a tribute
to his old humanitarian principles. 'You demand an exception to the death penalty in the
case of the one man to whom it legitimately
applies! Yes, speaking generally, the death
penalty is a crime, and for this reason that, according to the indestructible principles of nature, it can be justified only in cases in which
it is necessary to the security of individuals or
of the social body. But public security never
requires it in the case of ordinary crimes, be-

cause society can always prevent such crimes by other means, by putting the guilty party in the impossibility of doing further harm. . . . But Louis,' he said, returning to the subject of the debate, 'must die, because the fatherland must live.'

Let us not use the ridiculous term 'hypocrisy' that forms itself upon our lips almost automatically when we read logical nonsense of this kind. The passage might have been written by that great Victorian Mr. Lear, who would, however, have penned it more elegantly. For one thing, I doubt whether hypocrisy exists outside novels and books of edification. And, unlike Mr. Lear, Robespierre was not a humorist. He was profoundly sincere, on this as on all other occasions. He believed with all his soul that his humanitarian principles remained unimpaired. He had done his duty—a painful duty. When he noticed that Philippe Egalité, the *ci-devant* duke of Orleans, who had joined the Mountain and was a member of the Convention, voted for the death of his relative, he was very shocked. 'He could so easily have declared himself precluded from casting his vote,' he said. At the trial Robespierre spoke again, and once more he displayed that uncanny perspicacity that made him sense treason and plots. He pointed out that attempts at corruption were going on. The archives have since revealed how foreign influences and foreign gold were at work to buy the King's acquittal. But all was in vain, and Louis went to the scaffold on January 21, 1793.

Robespierre was mistaken, of course, when he thought that he would be able to maintain his opposition to the death penalty although he had voted for the death of the King. The idea of bloodshed was in the air. Then as in later ages war was familiarising men with violent death. Even before war had broken out, before common-law prisoners were massacred by the mob, while the King still resided in his palace of the Tuileries, people were talking of bloodshed and executions. No forcible revolution of human society can be made by those who hold human life to be sacred. Let me quote a few extracts from the correspondence of Edmond Géraud, a young man who was studying in Paris. His mentality was typical of the provincial bourgeoisie to which he belonged. In February 1792 he wrote to his father: 'Freedom can be saved only by two great evils: war or the flight of the King. I may even say that I ardently wish for one or other of these events to take place, for, as Mirabeau has foretold, our freedom can be secure only if it is allowed to rest upon a bed of corpses. . . .' More sedately, the father answered: 'If the crisis you think necessary must cause bloodshed, let us hope there will be no crisis.' Undaunted, the son retorted in his next letter: 'You have listened too much to the voice of humanity and to the generosity of your heart. But you cannot suspect me of being ferocious and bloodthirsty. Yet, even though it must lead to bloodshed, I call most ardently for the crisis which will restore freedom. Surely, you are aware that humanity and tolerance must keep silent when freedom speaks. You know that unhappily the price of freedom is blood. No, the time for clemency has not arrived. Let us first make the bases of our constitution secure.' The young man, who within a year had become a Girondin and an angry critic of Robespierre, ended with the inevitable reference to Sparta, Athens, and Rome.

Bloodlust had crept into the heart of France. It was in vain that Maximilien Robespierre tried to stifle it.

Events which it was beyond the power of

either the Gironde or the Mountain to influence settled two things: they made Robespierre obey, however reluctantly, and with many reservations, the almost universal clamour for blood, and they brought the struggle between Girondins and Montagnards to an issue. These events were in the first place military and political. They were also social: the spectre of famine and the resulting intensification of socialist agitation. At the end of February 1793 General Dumouriez invaded Holland. But March brought the first of a series of French defeats. On the 18th Dumouriez was beaten at Neerwinden, and he began the evacuation of Belgium. April came, and he went over to the enemy. At the same time the introduction of conscription met with opposition in many parts of France, and in Vendée the peasants rose just before the middle of March. There were terrible massacres of supporters of the central government. Noblemen and non-juring priests joined the revolt once it had started, and gave it a royalist and clerical character. Externally and internally, the new régime was in deadly danger.

When the first bad news arrived the Paris proletariat, led by the popular clubs, demanded the creation of an extraordinary tribunal that would judge without appeal all those guilty of anti-revolutionary enterprises, and of attempts to overthrow the republic. Danton supported these demands, and the Convention established the Revolutionary Tribunal, the instrument through which, in months to come, the Terror was to work. The only part Robespierre took in its creation was that he insisted upon greater precision in the text of the law in order to prevent the victimisation of good citizens. At the same time it was felt that the existing system of government, a ministry working under the supervision of the sovereign Convention, was not suited to a time of public danger. Various experiments were tried for putting the executive power in commission. In an attempt at conciliation a committee of twenty-five members was established at the end of March. Robespierre and several other Montagnards were given seats on it. But this unwieldy body functioned less than a fortnight. After the treason of Dumouriez a new committee, consisting of ten members, was formed, with the object of supervising the ministers. Dramatically, it was called the Committee of Public Safety (*Comité de Salut Public*). As months went by, the power of this committee increased. In July (1793) Robespierre joined it. By that time it was ruling France.

The recriminations and mutual accusations that followed the treason of Dumouriez brought about the final struggle between the two parties in the Convention. The press campaign against Robespierre reached an unprecedented degree of violence. He was called 'the viper of Arras,' 'the brood of Damiens the king-killer,' 'a man dried-up with his own venom, whose tongue is a dagger and whose breath is poison.' On their side, the deputies of the Mountain proposed a decree that would exclude from the Convention all deputies who had not voted for the immediate execution of Louis. To this direct attack the Girondins retaliated by decreeing the impeachment of Marat, the frenzied Montagnard who edited a fiery newspaper, *L'Ami du Peuple*. He was brought before the Revolutionary Tribunal, acquitted, and carried back shoulder high to the Convention. Other Montagnards were now arrested. A commission of twelve members was established by the Girondins to investigate a plot that the radical administration of the City of Paris, the Commune, was alleged to be hatching against the Convention. As a matter of fact the socialists were busy agitating, and the fears of the Girondins were by no means groundless. On May 25, Isnard, the Girondin who happened to be chairman of the Convention, threatened Paris with destruction. The following day a further batch of radicals were arrested. In the evening, at the Jacobins, Robespierre exclaimed: 'The people must rise, the moment has come!' It sounded a decisive call to direct action: at this moment he was undisputed leader of the left. The next day, the 27th, he tried to address the Convention on the subject of the arrests made by the commission of twelve. As in the old days of the Constituent Assembly, he was shouted down. As usual, the result was that he retired to meditate upon the situation and to prepare another speech. To deliver it he chose the platform of the Jacobins, where he appeared in the evening of the 29th. But now he was very vague indeed. 'I am incapable of prescribing for the people the measures by which they can save themselves,' he declared. 'Such capacity is vouchsafed to no one man. It has not been given to me, exhausted as I am by four years of revolution, and by the heart-rending spectacle of tyranny triumphing together with all that is most vile and corrupt. It has not been given to me, who am consumed by a slow fever, and especially by the fever of patriotism.' And so he spoke on, saying nothing, vague, abstract, dealing less with the situation than with Maximilien Robespierre, his disgust and his loss of heart.

At this critical juncture his indecision seems amazing. It smacks of timorousness. But one cannot possibly call Robespierre a coward. Only, he was not a man of action. He longed for another *journée,* but he was not the man to organise it. He knew it. And he also knew this danger of rousing the suburbs, the popular societies, the sections, where the socialists were in the ascendant. Robespierre did not see his way clearly; compared to oppression, insurrection appeared to be a lesser evil, but still an evil. Others were ready, however: the Paris proletariat, Marat. On the 31st the mob invaded the hall of the Convention. Vergniaud exclaimed that the debates were no longer free, and walked out. Nobody followed him. After a while he returned, and found Robespierre on the platform, free to speak, this time, because the hall was full of his supporters. *'Concluez donc!'* shouted Vergniaud. 'Yes, I will sum up,' replied Robespierre. 'I will sum up, and against you.' In a bitter, vehement peroration he demanded the immediate arrest of the twenty-two principal Girondin deputies. The Convention, with its majority still hesitating between the two factions, came to no decision. The agitation lasted throughout the following day, when the Convention did not meet. On June 2, while it was once more sitting, the crowd, led by Marat, again burst in, and this time, with the help of the Plain, a decree of accusation was passed against the principal Girondins. They were not treated harshly in this bloodless revolution. In theory, twenty-nine of them were consigned to their domiciles, but in fact they were left alone for the present. Twelve immediately fled to the provinces, eight more followed during the next few days.

The Mountain had conquered. The radicals were in power. 'The internal danger comes from the bourgeoisie. To defeat them, we must rally the people,' Robespierre scribbled in his pocket-book. But the task was not so simple. The people did not want quite the same things as Robespierre. And the Mountain was badly divided.

VII

AT HOME

THOSE citizens who had constituted themselves into a private bodyguard when the Girondin threats against Robespierre made them fear for his safety cannot have found their task particularly complicated. The habits of their hero were regular to the point of monotony, and except on rare occasions, all Paris knew where to find him at any hour of the day or of the night. Shortly after the massacres on the Champ de Mars (July 1791) he left his lonely rooms and settled with the family of the master-carpenter Duplay in the Rue Saint-Honoré. This fellow-Jacobin was one of Robespierre's innumerable admirers, and in the troubled days when the liberal majority of the Constituent Assembly were trying to make things unpleasant for the radicals he and his family invited Robespierre to join their establishment, not, indeed, in order to hide, but in order that he should never fail to be surrounded by a number of witnesses if an attempt were made to do him violence.

In our own period, which resembles that of the French Revolution in so many respects, this method is still useful in countries like Ireland and Germany where anarchy reigns.

Within a few weeks Robespierre discovered that he had found not only witnesses but warm-hearted friends and a home. The Duplays were kind and pleasant people. The father, who was in the middle fifties, had done well in business and become a small house-owner. His wife, three daughters and a son lived with him. Later a nephew, who had lost a leg in the battle of Valmy, joined them. He sometimes did secretarial work for Robespierre.

It pleased the disciple of Rousseau to be among simple people, while the puritan in him was more at home among the taboos and conventions of a lower-middle-class family than he would have been among proletarians. He also found and appreciated in the home of the Duplays certain joys he had hardly tasted in his youth: the maternal care of Madame Duplay, the merriness and familiarity of young girls. Among these people he allowed himself to unbend as he had done among the Rosatis at Amiens. He had his meals with them, and shared their life. They consulted him about everything, and they, in turn, protected his rare moments of leisure from the attempts of the outside world to invade his privacy. The scrutiny of four pairs of suspicious feminine eyes had to be braved before one could hope to have access to the tribune. They did not isolate him completely, however. Robespierre received more visitors than was realised at the time. For a dreamer he had his ears pretty close to the ground. Unless we believe him endowed with second sight, his natural suspiciousness is not sufficient to explain his uncanny gift for scenting plots and corruption that was so frequently justified by events.

When, before the days of the Convention, he had more leisure, Robespierre went out with the whole family for an occasional picnic at Montmorency or in the woods of Versailles. He also went to the theatre with them. During the last year of his life, when, apart from the Convention and the Jacobins, the meetings of the Committee of Public Safety took up much of his time, such excursions were hardly possible. But there were still walks in the Champs Elysées, when, carefully dressed as he always was, his Great Dane Brount following at heel, he walked with his friends towards a bench and gave small coins to the Savoyard urchins who played music and showed their marmots. Occasionally he visited friends. At one period he could be seen in the house of his colleague and former school-fellow Camille Desmoulins and of his blonde wife Lucille, holding on his knees their little son Horace.

After the family dinner he would adjourn with the Duplays to their drawing-room, which was full of his effigies, pictures, busts, reliefs and medallions, piously collected by the hosts. Usually he did not linger, because he had to hurry away to the Jacobins or to the Committee. But on Thursdays he was at home. Politicians, artists, and women-admirers called, sometimes in fairly large numbers. The politicians varied according to the friendships and alliances of the day. During the last year of his life young Saint-Just, whom we have already met, was frequently there, and so was Couthon, the radical lawyer with the paralysed legs, who had been a member of the Legislative Assembly and was now in the Convention. These two men shared Robespierre's political and philosophical views and eventually formed with him a group that dominated the Committee of Public Safety. Other visitors to the Thursday gatherings were the Montagnard painter David, and Buonarroti, pianist and social pioneer, collateral descendant of Michelangelo. Le Bas, a member of the Convention and son-in-law of the Duplays, sometimes sang or played the violin, accompanied by Buonarroti, who also performed compositions of his own. The conversation was usually general, and though politics were not avoided, it is natural that under Robespierre's guidance principles were discussed rather than their application. Besides, the private discussion of political tactics by members of the Assembly was still at that time considered a breach of morality of which only Girondins were capable. It required little pressure to make him dash upstairs and return with a volume of Rousseau's *La Nouvelle Héloïse* or with a play by Racine or Corneille, from which he read aloud to an admiring circle which was prone to shed a fashionable tear.

If all the Duplays liked him, Eléanore, commonly called Cornélie, somewhat masculine looking, restful rather than pretty, and then in her early twenties, felt for him something more than sisterly affection. It has been alleged that she was his mistress, but there are no grounds whatever for this assumption. In later years the survivors of the tragic family, two of whom, Madame Duplay and young Le Bas, shared Robespierre's fate, turned Eléanore into his fiancée. She may have had dreams of sharing the tribune's life when the revolutionary storm had dropped. It is not impossible that he reciprocated her feelings, but the evidence that there was an actual engagement is of the slenderest. Fervent idealism, and political activity reluctantly superimposed upon a natural bent towards speculation and criticism, were enough to fill Robespierre's life. He was never so fond of a human being as he was of Brount. Humanity he loved in the mass.

After the visitors had gone, or after his return from his evening meeting, Robespierre retired to his little room. There, among his familiar and simple furniture, he worked until the small hours, laboriously preparing his speeches and drafting his reports. With Brount at his feet he sat on a straw chair by his plain elmwood table. Three more straw chairs stood along the wall. There were some bookshelves made for him by Duplay, full of volumes of Rousseau, Voltaire, Montesquieu, Racine and Corneille, of papers and reports. The narrow bed made of walnut had striped curtains that came from

a dress Madame Duplay had worn. There
was only one window, which overlooked the
workshop. Often, in the early morning, the
sound of saw and plane warned him that it was
time to snatch a few hours of sleep.

Before tragedy put an end to the idyll it
was interrupted for a while by Robespierre's
domineering and ill-tempered sister Charlotte.
When their younger brother Augustine was
returned to the Convention by the electors of
Arras, she accompanied him to Paris and took
a couple of furnished rooms with the Duplays.
Soon she quarrelled with them and retired to
a flat of her own. Then she began a relentless
campaign to capture the tribune, of whom
she claimed to be the owner by right. Torn
between his dread relative and his beloved
friends, uncertain as ever about any problem
that had not been specifically solved for him
by Rousseau, the poor 'dictator' allowed himself to be kidnapped.

Charlotte was not an easy companion. She
wanted her great man to live in a style suited
to his position. She wanted her share of the
glory he was the last man to claim for himself.
She hoped to gather a salon about her and,
maybe, saw herself as another Madame Roland,

hostess and inspirer of the Mountain. But her cooking lacked the homeliness of that of Madame Duplay, and she could not tie Maximilien's complicated cravats like Eléanore and her sisters. She had known him so long; how could she have received his every word as an oracle? It put a strain upon him to answer her hysterical outbursts with the unruffled courtesy he invariably imposed upon himself. No longer did domestic serenity compensate for the tension and the violence of the day's work, and rest was needed more than ever, for it was in the days when the Girondin press campaign was at its worst. Robespierre fell ill. There was a raid in numbers by the Duplay clan. The strong man was captured and led away in triumph. With the hostage safe in their hands, the Duplays assumed the offensive. Maximilien was still ailing. Charlotte again called and criticised. One day she sent her servant with some preserves for the illustrious invalid.

'Take this stuff back to your mistress,' snorted Madame Duplay. 'Tell her I won't have Maximilien poisoned!'

Charlotte rose in her wrath and wrote a furious note. Henceforth, she could not even call. She transferred her affections to her second brother, Augustin Bon, who was so debonair that his friends called him *Bonbon*. Within a few months she managed to fall out with him also. But quiet reigned once more at the Rue Saint-Honoré. Maximilien, break-fasting in his dressing-gown with the Duplay girls, was again petted by them and by Madame. His cravats were as perfect as of yore. He had music and song, for which he did not care, and an ever-ready audience to whom he could read aloud to his heart's content.

VIII

CERTITUDE

Less than fourteen months were left to Robespierre. They were months of unconstitutional government, months when terrorism became an officially recognised system. They were months when the story of Robespierre and the history of France are almost inextricably mixed. Our task is to disentangle the two in so far as available evidence permits. We shall have to interpret the evidence, to make our choice between incompatible theories none of which lacks justification and plausibility.

We know what was done, we know Robespierre was one of the doers. Sometimes we know his share in the deed, more often we do not. We have his own utterances. We have the opinion of his innumerable adversaries, contemporary and posthumous. Documentary evidence bearing upon his case is to a large extent circumstantial. Were we primarily concerned with the history of France, we should find no difficulty in forming a judgment: the

main stream is never hidden. Personal motives
lose their significance when we consider the
map from above. But our biographical task is
specific and detailed, its very nature is to disentangle motives, intentions, aspirations. What
have we to guide us in our task?

There is the shape and essence of the mortal
soul of Robespierre. It was rigid, narrow, pure.
It had the immutability, the *sempiternum nunc*
with which the scholastics endowed their deity.
After June 2, 1793, he continued to be the
abstract lover of freedom, equality and virtue,
the unpractical theorist with a gentle nature
averse to violence, the passionate lover of consistency entirely unaware of his own limitations,
the Narcissus who worshipped his own past as
much as his own dandified appearance.

Character is sometimes altered by the stress
of events. Shakespeare ceases to be if we reject
mutability as an element in human behaviour.
There is conversion and rebirth. There is
panic. None of these, however, occurred in the
case of Robespierre. Nothing happened in
June 1793 or afterwards that could have caused
a sudden and fundamental revolution in his
temperament. The fall of the Gironde had
been triumphantly achieved after a long strug-

gle by a rising that met with his approval. It left him more powerful, but still a private member of the Convention. At the end of July he joined the Committee of Public Safety. This promotion, which he did not seek, which, indeed, frightened him, brought no giddy eminence, no irresistible temptation. It did not change him. If anything, it made him more profoundly conscious of the importance of immutability, so necessary to his self-esteem. His promotion took place without crisis or *coup d'état*. Within the Committee he persevered with the same task to which he had committed himself from the start. His immutability depressed his new eminence to the level of his former private position. Now, as before, he was the servant of an idea: the happiness of mankind could be achieved through a revolution inspired by the principles of Rousseau. He was the casket in which reposed the absolute revolutionary truth, and this knowledge preserved intact the blind self-confidence that was his in 1789 no less than in 1793.

Henceforth the National Convention, sovereign by the will—not too freely expressed—of the sovereign French nation, must be the instrument through which Robespierre was to work. It had been purified of reactionary Girondin elements by the revolutionary act of the nation on June 2. The nation, it is true, was represented merely by the Paris proletariat; dwellers in the absolute must sometimes content themselves with such symbolic approximations. The result was that in future no outside pressure upon the Convention could be justified. Unhappily, the Convention was still far from unanimous, far from perceiving the ultimate goal with the same distinctness of vision that had been vouchsafed to Robespierre. There were still moderates; a large number of leaderless Girondins had by now joined the shapeless Plain. The Mountain itself was not unanimous. It had triumphed, but it was not a party. It contained extremists who wanted what Robespierre wanted, but wanted it at once, without regard for the inertia of the outside world, with none of the elegance dear to him. And there were the easy-goers, lovers of the Revolution, but also of themselves, capable of compromise, of weakness, open to the temptations that come to members of the dominant faction in troublous times. Without premeditation, without love of power for its own sake, Robespierre found himself placed between these two tendencies. He made the discovery that he was a man of moderation, a Cicero, even before he had been invited to take a share in the government of the country. The discovery must have been painful to one who had given himself whole-heartedly to the Revolution. That there were also men who were not revolutionary enough, anti-revolutionary, perhaps, was nothing new to him. Had not his natural distrust always made him see indifference and treachery besetting freedom from its very birth in 1789?

Of course, he had to work the situation into a system. Nothing existed that could not be expressed in terms of a system. Through the endless number of formulations which he, unofficial and soon official formulator-in-chief of the revolutionary government, was going to pour out from the platform until two days before his death, the doctrine runs with deadly insistence. 'The agents of our enemies profess the principles of the Revolution only in order to assassinate it. Extravagant or moderate in turn, they preach weakness and sleep where vigilance and courage are required, temerity and exaggeration where prudence and circumspection are in their place,' he said. 'The waggon of the Revolution rolls upon uneven ground. Along easy ways they want to hamper its motion, on perilous roads they want to hustle it with violence. What they aim at is to break it against the final milestone.' Thus to act was false patriotism. How was it to be avoided? By vigilance, by purity, by genuine patriotism, in fact, although it was not put so bluntly, by agreeing with Robespierre. He knew his own honesty and revolutionary patriotism. He knew that he held the truth. *Ego sum via et veritas,* Messiah, Duce, Fuehrer. Such mysticism cannot be called ambition. It is the tragedy of certitude.

Others were certain too, but not so disinterestedly. The Girondin leaders whom Paris had rejected, and who fled to the provinces, raised rebellion. The Federalist insurrection affected sixty out of eighty-four départements. In the summer of 1793 the democratic revolution was in danger of death. Virtual leader of the Mountain, Robespierre rose in the Convention and demanded vigorous action. 'Let the knife fall upon the heads of the guilty!' he exclaimed (July 9). He had reconciled himself to the idea of death as the one means of defence left to the Republic. Yes, he had renounced his humanitarian opposition to the death penalty, but only for the duration of the war. The enemy within had to be killed like the enemy on the frontier: the executioner was a soldier. There should be no indiscriminate killing, however. Only those who were undoubtedly hostile to the Republic should be struck down.

With the Vendée still aflame, with the départements in rebellion, the northern frontier defence in imminent danger of collapse, those incredible men who were reshaping France made a new constitution. Robespierre took a leading part in the debates, but did not dictate. Many of his ideas, but not all, were adopted by the Convention. The constitution was never applied. It was suspended by common consent, and the Convention continued to govern through its committees. As we have seen, Robespierre was invited to join the Committee of Public Safety at the end of July. His moral power was immense; the Committee could not afford to allow him to remain a free-lance. They wanted him to share their responsibility. He knew he had no right to refuse.

The position of the Committee of Public

safety was anomalous and undefined. It represented the Convention and had the specific task of supervising the operations of the executive. It was responsible to the Convention for all its acts. It did not stand alone. By its side existed the Committee of General Security which supervised police, tribunals, and prisons. But gradually this committee was overshadowed by the other. The Convention, however, did not relinquish its own powers. It continued to debate, to control and even to quash decisions taken by the Committee of Public Safety. It continued to legislate and to decree on its own authority. But while it talked, the Committee worked. In its two daily meetings, held in the morning and in the evening, it governed France, directed the operations of the foreign and civil war, supervised the application of the law, organised the economic life of the nation.

Robespierre performed his share of the task. We do not know in every case what the share was. There are no minutes of the deliberations of the Committee, which were always held in secret. Decisions were signed by some of the members present, not necessarily by all. We know, among other things from his private note-book, that he initiated a certain number of civil and military measures. Nevertheless, he was in many respects a minister without portfolio, the spokesman of the Committee before the Convention and before the country. He was used as *agent de liaison* with the Jacobins. The government found the Jacobins useful, but was afraid of them. The best way to make them toe the line was to influence them through the mother society in Paris, which corresponded with all of them. And the way to influence the Paris Jacobins was to make them listen to Robespierre, whose abstract oratory, for some reason unfathomable to the modern reader of his speeches, filled them with transports of enthusiasm.[1]

As a Committee man Robespierre remained

[1] Here are two illustrations of Robespierre's methods and oratory. The first is from a speech on foreign affairs: 'Sublime Parliament of Great Britain, quote us the name of your heroes. You have an opposition party. Among you, patriotism is in opposition: this proves that despotism is triumphant. The minority is in opposition, therefore the majority is corrupt. Insolent and vile people, your pretended representation is venal under your eyes and to your knowledge. You even adopt the maxim that the talents of your deputies are an object of industry like the wool of your sheep and the steel of your factories. And you dare to talk of morality and freedom?' The other example: a deputy had written a report about the rebellious départements. Robespierre opposed those who wanted the report to be revised, and said: 'Either this report is good, or it is bad. In the first case it must be passed without modification, in the second there is no point in amending it.'

true to himself. No sooner was he appointed than he exposed the deficiencies of the Committee's procedure, just as in the summer of 1789 he had lectured the National Assembly about the inadequacy of its rules. He persuaded his colleagues to adopt new methods, to reorganise their clerical staff, to hold weekly joint meetings with the Committee of General Security. His colleagues knew what to expect of him: patient attention to minutiae, and an inexhaustible capacity to generalise. They made him write all the reports in which broad general principles had to be explained. These were the sermons and lectures that were distributed throughout the country, and read to the local assemblies of Jacobins, who listened to them with tear-stained eyes.

Sometimes we can look over Robespierre's shoulder and see him scribbling in his little note-book the innermost thoughts that came to him in his hours of meditation. 'A single mind is needed,' he once wrote. 'It must be either republican or royalist. If it is to be republican, we need republican ministers, republican newspapers, republican deputies, a republican government.' No more freedom of the press, no free representation in parliament.

Was this a betrayal of freedom? Certainly not; it was a curtailment of private freedom for the benefit of public freedom. As Saint-Just put it at a later date: 'institutions were needed that would make human pride bow for ever beneath the yoke of public liberty.' And all this was to be merely provisional, only while the crisis lasted, only until peace was achieved. Robespierre said so in many a speech. Have not all totalitarians started with emergency schemes which they afterwards attempted to make enduring? Robespierre, at any rate, was saved from temptation by death. There is no doubt whatever that he honestly saw the scheme as a purely temporary one. But totalitarian it certainly was. The Committee of Public Safety adopted it. In October, Saint-Just put it before the Convention, which forthwith sanctioned it. The government was to be revolutionary till the return of peace. It was not, strictly speaking, a dictatorship. The system had been practised for some time, and the Committee would continue, as before, to be responsible to the Convention. But it was agreed that there should be no elections, and that the new constitution should remain in abeyance.

The method through which the revolutionary government imposed its will upon the country is known to history as the Terror. There can be no doubt whatever that Robespierre was not an active agent in the establishment of this system, and that he did much to soften its application. But it is equally certain that he accepted it, and that on several occasions he assisted in sending people to the guillotine. In July (1793) the popular demagogue Marat was assassinated by a royalist woman. The Paris patriots demanded vengeance. In August the military situation grew worse. The road to Paris was open from the north. Lyons revolted. Toulon surrendered to the English, Corsica rose. There was scarcity in Paris, and apprehension of famine. From the Cordeliers and other popular societies, from the socialist and radical extremists in the Mountain, rose a cry for vigorous action. The Jacobins themselves were swept off their feet. 'Legislators,' they said in an address to the Convention, 'terror must become the order of the day.' The Convention gave way: while a vast and threatening delegation of Parisians looked on, it passed the decree demanded by the Jacobins. Robespierre was in the chair; he took no part in the debate (September 5).

Soon after, a further step was taken that gave more reality and horror to the system and made it hang as a threat over almost every home in France. A law was passed by the Convention declaring to be suspect, and as such liable to immediate arrest, all those who by their behaviour, connections, speeches and writings had shown themselves to be partisans of tyranny or federalism, and enemies of freedom. Suspect also would be all those whom the Convention had suspended from their functions, former noblemen, émigrés as well as their families and agents, and finally all those who had not constantly displayed their zeal for the Revolution. Again Robespierre took no part in the framing of this ghastly law, but he approved of it. He declared, however, that he wanted discretion in the application of it. The Revolutionary Tribunal, which had already functioned for some time, expedited its procedure. It was divided up in order to keep pace with its growing task. It worked not only for the repression of political enemies of the Revolution, but also for the punishment of people who endangered the national defence. Fraudulent army contractors were condemned to death. The extremists continually asked for more victims. Sometimes the Committee of Public Safety gave way to their pressure, as in the case of Queen Marie Antoinette, and of some of the Girondin leaders. The Tribunal could not move as fast as the local revolutionary committees that had everywhere been organised and were arresting suspects right and left. Soon the prisons were crowded beyond capacity. Still, the number of people who were executed was large enough. Before the death of Robespierre, in twelve months, the Terror killed almost as many victims in Paris as are killed in one year upon the roads of present-day England. The Terror was worse in some of the provinces, where deputies had been sent by the Convention to restore the rule of the Revolution. Sadists like Fouché at Lyons or Carrier at Nantes killed victims in their thousands, frequently without a show of legal process.

Up to the very end Robespierre tried to apply the brake. More than once he was successful. In October 1793 the Paris extremists demanded the execution of seventy-three deputies of the Girondin rank and file who were still in the Convention. They had signed a protest against the *coup d'état* of June 2 four days after it had taken place. The Convention, partly out of fear of the mob, wanted to hand them over to the Revolutionary Tribunal. It was a dramatic meeting: a motion had been passed forbidding any member to leave before the vote on the accusation had been taken. The prospective victims sat helpless among their fellow-members who were on the point of sending them to their death. Then Robespierre, who was just back from a sick-bed, rose and addressed the Convention in an impromptu speech. Amidst the hostile cries of the 'rabid' party he quietly lectured the Convention about the necessity of establishing a distinction between guilty people and people who had merely gone astray. Those who were not active enemies should be left untouched. Though he had every reason, he said, to hate the Girondins who had nearly made him one of their victims, these men should remain unharmed for the sake of keeping the Revolution alive. He carried the day: the seventy-three were saved. Later, when the terrorists had succeeded in putting them in prison (from where they emerged alive after the death of Robespierre), they sent him a collective letter in which they said: 'From the midst of the Convention we have carried into our captivity

a profound sense of gratitude for the generous opposition you formulated on Oct. 3 to the accusation made against us. Death will cause our hearts to wilt before the memory of your good action will be erased from them.' When in danger, the Girondin deputies used to write to Robespierre to appeal for his protection. When he fell, they were terrified and thought their last hour had come. The extremists, whose bloodthirst was insatiable, also clamoured for the execution of 28,000 people who in 1792 had signed a royalist petition. Again they found Robespierre in their path. More than once his colleagues on the Committee, and especially the rival Committee of General Security, thwarted his efforts to save innocuous victims from the executioner.

In two instances, however, Robespierre was on the side of the killers. This was in the spring of 1794, when a number of members of the right and of the left wings of the Mountain, including Hébert and Danton, were executed. Though for the sake of clearness we must deal separately with the victims on the right and those on the left, we shall have to remember that in Robespierre's mind it was impossible to distinguish between them, and that recent research has to a considerable extent proved this view to be correct. The 'rabid' section of the left pressed for executions among the right wing throughout the last quarter of 1793 and the first of 1794, and at the same time the right demanded punishment and execution for the extremists. Finally, the Committee of Public Safety had a number of both put to death. This was, if one likes, a somewhat elementary form of impartiality. In fact, considering the affair from the point of view of a Committee man inspired by the principles of provisional revolutionary government, it was an admission that there was much to be said for the allegations of both factions, and that their mutual accusations were not unfounded.

Let us first consider the agitation from the extreme left. It is interesting to note that with one at any rate of the principles for which it stood Robespierre was bound to feel much sympathy. The extreme left was socialist, and Robespierre was in favour of equality. Not, however, as we have already seen, to the extent of adopting the collectivist faith. While the Girondins were still in power (April 1793) he made a declaration that has often puzzled those who have since attempted to read his mind. He advocated the proclamation by the Convention of the following four points: '1. Property is the right of every citizen to enjoy and to dispose of the portion of goods that is guaranteed to him by law. 2. The right of property is limited, like all other rights, by the obligation to respect the rights of other people. 3. It must cause no prejudice to the security, the existence, the freedom or the property of others. 4. All trade that violates these principles is illegal and immoral.' Was this declaration made exclusively in order to buy the support of the extremists against the Girondins? No, because never in the whole course of his existence did Robespierre say a thing he did not believe. Was it then a declaration of socialist faith? Again no, for a careful reading of the four points and the fact that on the same occasion he also said that equality of property is a chimerical proposition prove that it was pure non-socialist radicalism such as still exists in France to-day.

At that period, in the first half of 1793, the socialists concentrated upon the demand for maximum prices kept artificially low at the tax-payer's expense, accompanied by rationing. In the midst of general shortage they used this agitation as a means to achieve eventual economic equality. The Jacobins, who were bourgeois, never agreed with the aims of this movement. But in so far as Robespierre could adopt some at any rate of the extremists' views without stepping beyond the frame-work of his own philosophy, he did so in order to make things difficult for his Girondin opponents. In May the Convention, still dominated by the Gironde, actually had to vote a maximum price for wheat. The maximum caused chaos and the disappearance of wheat from the markets. Where the Girondins had been compelled to give way it is not surprising that the Montagnard Committee of Public Safety, which stood so much nearer to the extremists, had to continue in the same direction. At the end of September, under pressure from the urban proletariat and part of the rural proletariat, the Committee proposed and the Convention passed a law applying maximum prices to all goods in France. Again, while the egalitarian Robespierre agreed, the anti-socialist Robespierre had his doubts. This time the doubts of the second Robespierre were reinforced by those of the Committee man who could not look at things merely through the glasses of theory. He was bound to see that these measures, so grudgingly granted by the Committee, were endangering the Revolution. The 'maximum' could not work. There was no telegraph, no possibility of thorough control of economic life from the centre of government.

Moreover, the men who were continually pressing for these measures of democratic economy were making themselves obnoxious in many other ways. They were greatly reinforced by the accession to their ranks of Hébert, always a radical, but not an extremist until he feared that common sense and moderation would make him lose his own particular following. Slight and small, with white, delicate hands, highly cultured, refined in manners, this strange man edited the vilest conceivable newsrag, the *Père Duchesne,* written for the Paris workmen in the most astonishing prose, peppered with slang, oaths, and indecent words. He hoped to become the successor of Marat. He demanded the guillotine even for shopkeepers, insisted upon the extension of the Terror, and preached violent insurrection to the masses. A special legion called the Revolutionary Army had been founded by the Convention, also under extremist pressure, in order to search for food and produce in the countryside. 'When a detachment of the Revolutionary Army comes to a village,' the Hébertist Brichet said at a meeting of the Jacobins, 'it must enquire whether the local farmer is rich. If the answer is yes, let him be guillotined at once. He is sure to be a monopolist.'

The Hébertists shocked Robespierre by their language. They shocked him still more by launching a systematic campaign for the dechristianisation of France. Encouraged by Hébert, representatives on mission in the provinces persecuted priests and demolished church steeples as being an offence against equality. The result was the alienation of vast masses of Catholics from the Revolution. The Committee was alarmed. It was one of those cases when the pen of Robespierre was clearly needed. He wrote in the name of the Committee to one of these anti-christian missionaries: 'You have struck too violently against the objects of Catholic worship. Do not provide hypocritical anti-revolutionaries with pretexts that seem to justify their calumnies. Do not apply to regions where patriotism is lukewarm those violent remedies necessary only in rebellious parts. Be gentle towards the weak and ignorant masses.' But the power of the Committee or of its spokesman hardly extended beyond their physical horizon. The campaign went on, sacred vessels were confiscated and melted down, and the precious metal thus obtained did not always find its way to Paris. A new revolutionary calendar was introduced at the behest of the Hébertists. It established one day of rest in ten and did away with Sundays. Many churches were closed or used for worldly purposes. In some mock religious ceremonies were held, such as that of November when the goddess of reason was adored at Notre Dame in Paris. Robespierre's brother Augustin returned from a five months' mission in the provinces and told tales of the harm done by the Hébertists, especially by their religious policy. Maximilien himself saw the dangers of the movement; but he also disapproved of it on principle. He believed in a supreme being, an active providence, and preferred this being to be served superstitiously rather than that it should be denied or mocked. He made several speeches against the new paganism and reminded his hearers that freedom of worship was guaranteed by the constitution.

Meanwhile it was becoming clear that the maximum-price regulations of the Hébertists had led nowhere. Hébert attributed this failure to the sabotage of the Committee, and clamoured for more violence and more blood. His partisans incited the mob to massacre prisoners as had been done in September 1792. They called Robespierre and his supporters the party of *endormeurs* (dope-merchants). Again the Committee of Public Safety offered concessions, but once more these concessions fitted in with Robespierre's theories. Towards the end of February (1794) a decree was passed confiscating the goods of the arrested suspects in order that they should be distributed to poor patriots. It was a big measure of social levelling which, if applied, would have created a new group of small landowners. It took the wind out of Hébert's sails. He became more violent still, and attacked Robespierre at the Cordeliers in a speech ending with the words: 'Insurrection, yes insurrection!' Whereupon the Cordeliers proclaimed themselves to be in a state of insurrection (March 4, 1794). Robespierre was ill, but in close touch with the Committee. He agreed that the Hébertists must be arrested, not, indeed, because of their politics, but because they were preparing a coup. There was another reason for immediate action. The opponents of the Hébertists, the party of the easy-goers, also looked like becoming more dangerous. It was decided to strike out at both left and right, and if the blow to the left fell first, it was because the left was itself ready to strike.

The deputies of the Mountain who stood to the right of Robespierre and the Committees were even less a party than the *exagérés*. They were a mixed crowd inspired by no common ideal and not even united by common interests. There were men involved in army contracts, or connected with contractors whom they protected and from whom they received bribes. There were speculators and friends of speculators. The most astounding scandal in which some of them became involved was that of the India Company, of which the shares were first depressed by an unscrupulous campaign in the papers and from the platform of the Convention, while afterwards an attempt was made to send them up again by the actual falsification of a decree of the Convention. By patient archive work Mathiez has been able to unravel much of the amazing corruption that went on during the Terror. We can no longer doubt the guilt of a number of deputies of the right wing of the Mountain.

Contemporaries were aware of what was going on. The meetings of the Convention and of the Jacobins often resounded with impassioned appeals for the punishment of men who were called *les pourris* (the rotten ones). Frightened accomplices who saw themselves in imminent danger approached members of the Committees and made half-admissions in the hope of escaping punishment. The Hébertists were wakeful and demanded the death penalty against the guilty. These men, in their turn, fought the Hébertists tooth and nail, and asked for their execution as a preliminary to a milder system of government. In October, Fabre d'Eglantine, who afterwards proved to be one of the corrupt deputies, was able to gain the confidence of Robespierre and thus to cause the temporary arrest of a number of Hébertists.

To Robespierre, as we have already seen, and to the other members of the Committees also, exaggeration and indulgence seemed to be two aspects of treason, both inspired by hatred of the Revolution. As early as September 1793 the deputy Julien, of Toulouse, knowing that some of his unsavoury operations were on the point of being discovered, mounted the platform of the Convention and proposed in all seriousness to make the wearing of the red-white-and-blue cockade compulsory for all women, the punishment for a first neglect to be eight days' imprisonment, and for the next the placing of the offender on the list of suspects, *i.e.* of candidates for the guillotine. The Committee knew that such exaggerations were welcomed by the enemy Powers, that the English government used the utterances of the rabid party as propaganda material. Proofs were even discovered that in a few instances foreign agents had actually encouraged excess in order to unnerve the Revolution.

It is interesting to observe, meanwhile, that if, intellectually and in the abstract, the social programme of the left extremists inspired one part of Robespierre with sympathy, he was by temperament attracted by the propaganda in favour of mildness conducted by some of the right-wing opposition. If the *pourris* favoured mildness in order to save their own skins, their

appeals found an echo in the minds of some
people who were moderate by nature and
wanted mildness for its own sake. More than
once Robespierre came down on their side.
We mentioned Julien of Toulouse, the en-
thusiast of the national cockade. In the
middle of October (1793) he had become
highly suspect, and Robespierre had heard
something of his dealings with a dishonest
contractor, the Abbé d'Espagnac. He decided
to give Julien a rough but salutary warning.
In a speech before the Convention he accused
him of having written a report that was reactionary and aristocratic. 'In the midst of
the Mountain,' he said, pointing at Julien,
'I can see men who are ready to assassinate
the fathers of liberty!' The Hébertist Brichet
rose and demanded the immediate arrest of
Julien. 'It is only with regret,' replied Robespierre, 'that I have denounced a report
written by a man whom I have seen for a long
time walking along a line parallel to that
favoured by the best patriots. There is no
question therefore of arrest and guillotine.
What we are concerned with is to save freedom
by wise measures.' Julien thereupon ascended
the platform and confessed that he had been

careless. No action was taken until a few months later, when details of his dishonest dealings came to light. On another occasion, in January 1794, when the deputy Fabre d'Eglantine was defending himself at the Jacobins against various accusations, a member interrupted him with the cry 'To the guillotine!' Robespierre expressed his indignation and demanded that the interrupter should be expelled from the club. A vote was immediately taken and Robespierre's proposal was carried out. Fabre was allowed to proceed with his defence, and no decision was taken. But a few days later the Committee of General Security had him arrested in connection with the affair of the India Company.

Robespierre, however, had not been converted to a policy of universal mildness. He tried to judge each case on its own merits. Like his colleagues on the Committees, he felt himself placed between two fires, and acquired a growing certainty that both were fanned by the same hand. While the ultra-terrorist, socialist, and anti-religious work of the left was carried on in the open, the right-wing opposition operated stealthily but indefatigably. At the Jacobins and in the Convention its supporters denounced the men in power; they wormed their way into the Committees; they distracted the attention of the Robespierrist Committee men by making them afraid for their own safety. It is only natural that in the end the Committees became convinced that whoever criticised them was corrupt and an agent of the enemy. Such a belief was most natural in Robespierre, always full of suspicion and convinced that his own formula was correct. Nervousness, suspicion, naïve self-confidence, a fatal tendency to systematise and to correlate incompatibles, but also the tangible existence of corruption and treason—did not a diplomatic agent of the Republic forward to the Committee a complete report of one of their secret meetings obtained from an enemy diplomat?—such are the explanations of the drama that reached its climax in March 1794.

The first hostile group to be arrested, as we have seen, was composed of men of the left. During the night of March 13-14 Hébert and a number of his friends were rounded up. The next day Robespierre addressed the Convention: 'All factions must perish at one blow!' he exclaimed. The Convention voted that the prisoners should be sent before the Revolutionary Tribunal; their trial began on the 21st, they were beheaded on the 25th. Six days later the second blow fell: a batch of members of the right-wing opposition were arrested.

The execution of these alleged advocates of humaner government is held up against Robespierre as the main proof of his cruelty and bloodthirstiness. Certainly the episode was gruesome. Camille Desmoulins, who was among them, had been a friend of Robespierre. Danton, the principal victim, is considered by many as the greatest hero of the Revolution. And the methods adopted at the trial of these men turned it into a parody of justice. In favour of Robespierre it may be argued that once the principle of revolutionary or emergency government was admitted, these men and most of their fellow-victims were guilty and dangerous, and had to be removed from the political scene. Could they not have been kept in prison instead of being sent to the scaffold? But in those days, when communal life among prisoners was the rule, intrigue would have been difficult to prevent. At the first *journée* an alternative government would have emerged from prison. As in the King's trial, justice was not the main consideration:

there was a life-and-death struggle, in which
the Dantonists had to be crushed. Thus, at
any rate, did the Committee men picture the
situation. It is also true that, as far as Danton
was concerned, a fair trial would have been
dangerous. His irresistible eloquence might
sway the jury; as in the case of Marat there
might be an acquittal, and this would have
been the end of the revolutionary system.

The case of Camille Desmoulins is pathetic.
Light-hearted, witty, devoted to his older
school-fellow Robespierre, who had been a
witness at his wedding, Camille supported the
policy of the Committees until he airily
fluttered into the company of *indulgents* and
pourris. In his paper *Le Vieux Cordelier* he
opened a campaign in favour of mildness.
Robespierre began by approving of it until he
acquired the conviction that mildness and
corruption went hand in hand. But Camille
went farther than Robespierre could possibly
go. Soon he was criticising the whole theory
of revolutionary government in articles that
delighted the royalists and reactionaries. He
was attacked at the Jacobins. Robespierre
defended him. He was attacked again and
expelled from the club. Again Robespierre

spoke in his favour and persuaded the club to readmit him, thus providing the *exagérés* with a new grievance against himself. When finally, in March, it had been decided to take action against the *indulgents*, Robespierre's colleagues added Camille's name to those of the victims, and Robespierre, hardening his heart, consented.

Danton, as has already been mentioned, had been bribed by the Court in earlier days. He dabbled in various conspiracies, and was almost certainly implicated in the plot of General Dumouriez, who tried to play the Bonaparte be-before the time was ripe for a military dictatorship. With the guile of a peasant he avoided committing himself before the event, and he was able to disentangle himself when Dumouriez failed and surrendered to the enemy. As a commissioner in Belgium he was guilty of highly undignified behaviour at a time when it was essential to respect the susceptibilities of a religious population, and he tried to smuggle into France cartloads of looted silver and table-linen. He was the friend of people whom he knew to be guilty of financial corruption. In many other ways he acted most suspiciously. While the Committee of Public Safety strained every nerve to defend the country against a foreign invasion which, if successful, would have destroyed the republican régime, Danton worked privately for a peace by compromise. Rightly or wrongly, this kind of private war-time diplomacy is considered punishable in our own days. His was a mobile, restless mind, ever ready to try new schemes, to readjust his ideals to the needs of the moment. He was an opportunist. Had he been a trifle less indifferent and lazy, he might, like Fouché, have weathered the storm and become an admirable Napoleonic minister.

Robespierre disliked Danton. His loose-living shocked the puritan. His conversation was Rabelaisian. Once he chided Robespierre for his fondness of the word virtue. 'There is no virtue more solid,' he said, 'than that I display every night with my wife.' Yet, though he disliked him, Robespierre recognized the great services he had rendered to the Revolution. As attacks upon Danton at the Jacobins increased in number, Robespierre took his defence more than once.

It was actually a few days before the arrest of the Hébertists that the Committee of Public Safety began to prepare its case against the men

of the right. It took Robespierre's colleague
Billaud-Varenne, whom Camille Desmoulins
had dubbed the bilious patriot, several days to
convince him that Danton was the principal
enemy. At last he believed Varenne, and was
handed a report against Danton, written by
Saint-Just. He read it and began to make
annotations, to correct its style, suppress pas-
sages here and there, and add a few remarks.
As he went on his pen began to move faster.
His fundamental dislike of Danton had the
better of him. He scribbled away his passionate
distrust of the jovial, unchaste fellow, who
lacked culture and general ideas about the
Revolution, his hatred for the compromiser
and the thief, his resentment at having protected him so long. He added new grievances
and further accusations.

Armed with these notes, Saint-Just rewrote
his report and read it before the Convention.
Robespierre pronounced a vehement speech
against Danton and the others, and carried a
vote of accusation. The Dantonists were prevented from defending themselves in the
Convention. Before the Tribunal their defence
was also stifled. Members of the Committee
saw the jury privately and brought to bear

further arguments against the accused which had not been included in the public indictment. Danton roared a protest and was dragged away. He died theatrically, magnificently, appealing to posterity. Camille Desmoulins cried.

IX

DOUBTS

APRIL, May, June, July of 1794 were months of real dictatorship. It was never the dictatorship of a single man, least of all of Robespierre. The Committee of Public Safety and the Committee of General Security existed side by side; some twenty men shared power. They had destroyed the strongest personalities among their opponents, but, though driven underground, the opposition continued. Indulgence had been cowed; extremism, if careful not to come out into the open, had many supporters nevertheless. Terror remained the system of government. Lucille Desmoulins, the widow of Camille, went to the scaffold on a trumped-up charge of having attempted to foment a conspiracy against the Committees in the prisons of Paris. But as soon as the Hébertists had gone down, the Committee of Public Safety decided to slacken the pace in one respect. The guillotine ceased to be used in support of economic radicalism. Without rescinding maximum-price regulations the Committee began to encourage freedom of trade; the initiative came from Robespierre. Couthon and Saint-Just, though in general his closest associates, were more socialistic than his own respect for the principle of property allowed him to be.

The revolutionary army, that body of rummaging volunteers who were supposed to enforce rationing and maximum-prices in the countryside, was disbanded. Commerce was no longer to be treated as an enemy. 'Hébert,' said Robespierre, 'declared some time ago that trade was despotism. This implied that trade was a crime. Our enemies wanted to destroy our trade in order to bring famine to our people and to reduce them to servitude by hunger.' Surplus stocks were exported to neutral countries, instead of being sold to the people at a loss.

The return to orthodox economic practice had an interesting repercussion. When the general maximum for prices was proclaimed, a maximum for salaries and wages was also established. But while Hébertism was strong no attempt was made to apply it. After the March executions the Committee of Public

Safety decided that it should be enforced. Owing to labour shortage it proved more difficult to maintain low wages in private enterprise than in the munitions and other state factories. To this end the freedom of the workers was seriously curtailed. The Convention prohibited the offering or demanding of wages above the fixed maximum, even in the case of agricultural labourers, and workers were allowed to meet for the discussion of their interests only after permission had been granted in each case by the authorities. The result of this decree was a series of strikes, which were repressed with much severity. The Cordeliers and other popular societies were dissolved. A number of unruly agricultural labourers were arrested as suspects.

Far from being socialistic, the Committee of Public Safety was evolving towards what is nowadays called the totalitarian conception of the state. The press lost every vestige of freedom. Only semi-official and inspired publications were allowed. The only clubs that were not closed were those of the Jacobins, and thus the Committee had its fascist cells, censoring, raiding, and supervising all citizens. The Convention became an organ for registering the decisions of the Committees. Descriptions of the economic dictatorship exercised by the Committees, their efforts at centralisation, the cultivation of waste lands, the war against idleness, compulsory work on the roads, all read like contemporary history. Nationalism, the inseparable twin of totalitarianism, was officially encouraged. 'I hate the English people!' Robespierre had exclaimed a few months earlier, and speeches on this theme were heard periodically at the Jacobins and spread through their affiliated societies. The great national effort made under the inspiration of government-fostered chauvinism began to bear fruit. In the early spring of 1794 the French armies resumed their victorious advance.

Totalitarianism calls for a state religion. In providing for this need Robespierre was in his element, because policy coincided with his dearest theories. The proclamation by the Convention that the French nation recognised the existence of a Supreme Being and the immortality of the soul was his work. Politically, the systematic destruction of Christianity had been one of the most dangerous activities of the Hébertists. Robespierre, who, as we saw,

149

fought dechristianisation on grounds of policy as well as of principle, would have preferred to see the end of Christianity, but not before a long preparation had made people ready for the change, and especially not before something concrete could be evolved to replace the old religion. In common with most if not all the philosophers of the eighteenth century, he considered that the masses needed religion, and that the best religion was one in which State and Church, instead of being rival powers, were identified. Convinced himself of the existence not only of spiritual values but of a concrete deity that took a direct interest in human affairs, he decided upon a system in which his philosophy, the interest of the state and the aspirations of the bulk of the nation would find joint expression. As usual, he did not invent. He helped himself from what had already grown under the new régime. The Jacobins and the popular societies were fond of ritual and symbolism. Solemn patriotic celebrations in honour of republican virtues and patriotic ideas had sprung up everywhere. All these ceremonies, spontaneously evolved by a people that had suddenly been deprived of one of the most ritualistic forms of worship ever known in

Europe, Robespierre wove into a new religion of which he made himself the prophet.

On May 7, in the name of the Committee of Public Safety, he addressed the Convention in a carefully studied speech, full of classical allusions and illustrations from Greek and Roman history, and advocated the establishment of a national religion in honour of the Supreme Being, with numerous festivals for the celebration of virtue, freedom, truth, pudicity, immortality, friendship, disinterestedness, youth, old age, and many other abstractions. He declared that immorality was the basis of despotism, virtue the essence of republicanism. Atheism, being the parent of vice, was an invention of despotism for the corruption and undoing of the Republic. The Republic must therefore fight atheism and worship the Supreme Being. Collective festivals were justified in these words: 'Make men forgather, and you will improve them; for when in company men will try to please one another, and they can only please by what makes them worthy of esteem. Give to their gatherings a great moral and political motive, and the love of honourable things will enter their hearts at the same time as pleasure. For men do not meet without experiencing pleasure.' It has been already pointed out to what extent we liberalised Westerners have lost touch with the mentality of the French Revolution. The duller a speech of those days appears to us, the more certain of success it seems to have been at the time it was delivered. The Convention listened enthralled, punctuated Robespierre's words with applause, adopted unanimously a decree granting all the things he asked for, and ordered the printing and broadcasting of his speech. In the evening the Jacobins clamoured for an encore, and the scenes of enthusiasm of the afternoon were re-enacted at the club.

The festival of the Supreme Being, the first celebration to be held under the new decree, took place on June 8. Crowds that had flocked to Paris mingled with Parisians in a festive mood. Houses were adorned with bunting and foliage; the day was fine. At the usual monthly election Robespierre had been made chairman of the Convention, no doubt in order that he might preside at his festival. Arriving near the hall where the Convention was assembling, Robespierre pointed towards the crowd and said to an acquaintance: 'Look, here is the most interesting portion of mankind. The Universe is assembled here. O Nature, how sublime and delicious is thy power! How the tyrants must pale at the thought of this celebration.' This casual remark indicates the key in which the celebration, organised by the painter David, was held. The members of the Convention filed out, each carrying a bouquet composed of flowers, ears of corn, and fruit. They were dressed in a ceremonial costume, uniform in cut, but each member had chosen the colour he fancied. Robespierre wore yellow breeches and a blue coat. Outside the building a tall cardboard monument representing atheism had been erected. Robespierre made a speech, after which he was handed a flaming torch; to the accompaniment of music he set fire to the 'idol.' From the midst of the flames rose a statue of wisdom, pointing one hand heavenward and clasping a crown of stars in the other. Then he made a second speech, religious and patriotic like the first. A procession now moved to the Champ de Mars. It was headed by a group of old people. Then, in succession, came mothers, children, maidens, and the Convention, its chairman walking gravely in front. Upon the Champ

153

de Mars stood an artificial hillock, representing the Mountain. A regrettable conflict of historical testimony makes it impossible to ascertain whether Robespierre pronounced a third speech. We do know that a vast choir sang a lengthy hymn to the Supreme Being.

The crowd cheered Robespierre, who, though not the head of the government, was undoubtedly its figurehead. But in the ranks of the Convention there were murmurs. Some of those who had applauded his speeches most frantically were least pleased with the new religion. They were the cowed survivors of Hébertism, atheists, ultra-terrorists, the proconsuls who had spread desolation in the provinces. They knew Robespierre had his eye upon them, they knew that he still wanted to restrict the Terror. He had hopes of applying it henceforth to conspirators only, to avowed supporters of royalism. But he knew that there were opponents to a régime of mildness, and these opponents he wanted to silence by means of the only instrument that imposed eternal silence. When the Hébertist leaders were executed he caused the arch-terrorist Fouché to be recalled to Paris. There had been a dramatic meeting at the Jacobins.

Criticised by his fellow-members, Fouché tried to put the whole blame upon Chaumette, one of the executed Hébertists. Robespierre read him a lesson in his usual tone: 'It will not do to throw mud at the tomb of Chaumette after this monster has perished on the scaffold. It would have been better to fight him while he was alive. Too long has harm been done by those who speak the language of republicans. . . . There are men who seem all aflame for the defence of the Committee of Public Safety while they are sharpening their daggers against it!' Fouché had not forgiven these words. Besides, he was afraid. This made him more dangerous still.

Shortly before the festival of the Supreme Being a dismissed clerk with a personal grievance tried to kill Robespierre. On the following day an hysterical girl attempted to get near him. She was arrested. Two small knives were found in her pocket. Was it another attempt on his life? Were his opponents trying to frighten him into measures that would have given him the air of a tyrant? At any rate, when the Jacobins congratulated him on his escape and offered to give him a bodyguard he declined, saying that this would merely encourage those who talked about tyranny. He brushed aside like a pestilent thing a mere symbol of tyranny, because, like his contemporaries, he attached more importance to symbols than to realities. But almost at the same time he proposed a measure which, far more than the possession of a bodyguard, had the appearance of being the real thing.

The festival was hardly over when he persuaded the Convention to pass a decree by which the right to defend themselves was withdrawn from all persons brought before the Revolutionary Tribunal. His main purpose was to strike with greater vigour and certainty at the atheists and ultra-terrorists. With his naïve belief in the fundamental goodness of men he fondly imagined, as did his friend Couthon, that patriotic jurymen would be able to detect error if it crept into the accusation, and to judge the accused by patriotic intuition. Alas, the Convention did not share his illusion. It passed the decree, but it had the hardihood, a few days later, to criticise the new procedure. Robespierre had to defend it again. He spoke, sure of the purity of his intentions, unable to understand that criticism or opposition might be due to other than anti-revolutionary motives. He explained that there were only two parties in the Convention, good citizens and bad citizens. How could one fail to distinguish them! 'The Mountain is pure!' he exclaimed, 'the Mountain is sublime! The intriguers are not of the Mountain!' 'Name them!' shouted a deputy. 'I shall name them when it becomes necessary,' retorted Robespierre. And thus scores of deputies were left in uncertainty, each one imagining that he might be the next victim of the Terror. It was an amazing blunder on the part of a man who has been called a scheming and calculating politician. He repeated it two months later. Then he paid for it with his life.

Fear was the main inspiration of the underground opposition, which increased daily in volume. There was fear among the few whom the revolutionary government really threatened, the neo-Hébertists Fouché, Barras, Tallien, and also among those who during the tragic days of March had barely escaped being involved with the other *exagérés*. But there were other opponents, inspired by a variety of motives: those who were jealous of Robespierre's moral influence; those whose material interests from the maximum regulations still maintained even if less strictly applied; those who were tired of the war; honest and decent people who hated terrorism and who, justifiably misled by appearances, believed that Robespierre wanted to intensify the Terror. All these men felt a common desire to see the end of the rule of the Committee of Public Safety. The Committees themselves were disunited. The Committee of General Security had developed the professional mentality of police chiefs and objected to a decrease of terrorism. It was on the side of Fouché. Inside the Committee of Public Safety, overworked and personally threatened men with frayed nerves had come to hate each other. Even faithful Saint-Just had a momentary quarrel over military matters with Robespierre.

In order to weaken Robespierre's position the Committee of General Security staged a prosecution against a group of silly women led by a certain Catherine Theot, who called herself the Mother of God and conducted queer ceremonies at which she prophesied to her followers. The group was arrested on the charge of counter-revolutionary activities, and in the course of the investigations that followed a letter from Catherine Theot was found, addressed to Robespierre, in which he was called 'Son of the Supreme Being, Eternal Verb, Redeemer of Mankind, Messiah.' The letter was almost certainly a forgery. But it placed Robespierre before a serious dilemma. If the accused were convicted and executed, he would seem to have allowed them to go to their death because they had made him ridiculous. If he saved them from the scaffold he could be said to acknowledge them as his supporters, or at least to have basked in their adulation. He bravely chose the humaner alternative, saved them from the guillotine after a hard fight with the Committee of General Security, and became the man who protected those who called him the Son of God.

In his bitterness he ceased to attend the meetings of the Committees, and took no part in public business for four weeks. Once more he acted as no man would who aimed at dictatorship. He nursed his wounded pride, walked in the Champs Elysées with his dog Brount, wrote copious notes, and waited, it would be hard to say for what. Meanwhile his enemies had a clear field. They circulated a list which they said had been drawn up by him, and which contained the names of a number of the most innocuous members of the Convention. This was supposed to be the list of those against whom he had addressed his vague and clumsy threat. Some of the supposed victims were so frightened that they slept away from their homes. A large number of deputies were persuaded that their only chance was the death of the tyrant. But, though the tyrant was away, the Terror went on. Innocent people were arrested, and cartloads of victims were daily taken to the scaffold.

Some members of the Committees, knowing Robespierre's popularity with the Jacobins and other militant revolutionaries, decided to bring about a reconciliation. Unless Robespierre were placated the Convention would have to arbitrate, for in theory it was still the supreme authority. Therefore, on July 22, in the month of *Thermidor* by the new calendar, Robespierre was invited to attend a joint meeting of the two Committees, where it would be proved to him that they intended faithfully to apply the new system of revolutionary jurisdiction he had sponsored. He appeared the following day. The atmosphere, rather chilly at first, was considerably warmed by a speech of Saint-Just, who said that as the continuance of the system of revolutionary government was a *sine qua non* of victory, union must at all costs be restored in the Committees. They knew, he said, that Robespierre had not aimed at a dictatorship. How could he have done, since he had no control of the armed forces, of national finance, or of the administration? Then Robespierre was invited to reply. Once more that schemer, that far-sighted leader of men, blundered. He allowed the bitterness of his heart to overflow. He was sarcastic, he become personal. He said that he would appeal to the Convention against all intriguers, those within the Committees as well as those outside. He threatened to do the very thing his colleagues had hoped to avoid by convening this meeting. They parted without anything having been achieved.

On July 28, Robespierre appeared before the Convention. He made a long speech, the ablest among those of his that have been preserved. It was, as he had threatened, an appeal from the Committees to the Convention, and a philippic against the ultra-terrorists. He complained of the persecution to which he was subjected, and confessed that his reason, though not his heart, was on the point of doubting the possibility of the virtuous republic he had planned. But once more his dislike of immediate decisions, his craving for leisure in which to consider problems from every conceivable angle, made him commit the mistake of uttering vague general accusations. He refused to give the names of those who were his enemies and therefore those of the Republic. 'I dare not name them at this moment and in this place. I cannot bring myself entirely to tear asunder the veil that covers this profound mystery of iniquity. But I can affirm most positively that among the authors of this plot are the agents of that system of corruption and extravagance, the most powerful of all the means invented by foreigners for the undoing of the Republic, I mean the impure apostles of atheism and of the immorality that is at its basis.' Had he not spoken these words he might still have triumphed. Once more he received the applause to which he was accustomed. But after the first enthusiasm the Convention began to wonder at whom the speech was aimed. Instead of granting him its unqualified support it decided that his accusations should be investigated by a commission.

That night many members of the Convention did not sleep in their beds. Fouché and the other terrorists went about saying that Robespierre wanted unlimited powers in order to strike at whomever his sanguinary fancy might happen to pick out. The Plain agreed to join in an attack, the chairman of the Convention promised his support. When the meeting of the Convention opened, Saint-Just went to the platform to speak in support of Robespierre. He was interrupted and shouted down, while anti-Robespierrists were allowed to speak freely. Robespierre tried to answer, but he too was silenced. Several members in the body of the hall rose simultaneously to demand his arrest. The chairman at once put the proposal to the vote. It was carried. Augustin Robespierre rushed to the platform and cried that he wished to share the fate of his brother. His arrest was voted, and a decree of accusation was also carried against Couthon, Saint-Just, and Le Bas, the son-in-law of Robespierre's hosts. They were immediately arrested. On receiving the news the radical administration of Paris, the Commune, called for an insurrection. Its supporters liberated the prisoners and carried them off to the Town Hall (where Robespierre made a speech). These actions were spontaneous, and since the beginning of the French Revolution no coup had been successful unless it had been carefully prepared. The proletariat, moreover, was not unanimous in its support of the Commune, because many workers resented the maximum-wage policy. The rebels lacked supporters, staying power, and a plan.

The Convention, however, was acting. It outlawed the escaped prisoners, which meant that if caught, they could be executed without judgment. In the more conservative sections of Paris the national guards were called up. Preparations were made for marching against the Town Hall. There Robespierre's friends were drawing up an appeal for the support of the section to which Robespierre belonged and which was very radical. For a long time he could not bring himself to approve of this step. It is not that his legal mind refused to sanction an unconstitutional deed, as has sometimes been said in explanation of his indecision. He had preached rebellion on more than one occasion. But his certitude

had left him. He had always identified himself with the Revolution. The two great
abstractions he worshipped were the Nation
and the Law. The legal organ of the Nation,
the Convention, whose authority he had never
denied, to which only yesterday he had appealed against his enemies, had outlawed him.
Now he stood outside the Law, outside the
Nation. He, who used to think of himself
as the Law, began to wonder. The absolute
had ceased to be identical with himself.

His friends urged him to face the facts.
The Convention had cast him out. Let him
be a rebel. Let him add his name to the
appeal, as they had already done. 'Sign,'
they said. 'In the name of whom? In the
name of what?' he asked, bewildered. At
last, still unconvinced, he gave way to their
pressure. He began to sign. On the blood-
stained document that still exists the first two
letters only of his name appear. Did his
doubts prevail? Did he throw down his pen?
Or was it 2 o'clock in the morning, the moment
when the troops of the Convention reached
the Town Hall, and meeting with no resistance,
entered the room where the outlaws were in
conference? A pistol shot rang out. Robes-

pierre dropped on the table. We do not know whether he tried to commit suicide, or whether a member of the attacking party shot him. The bullet entered one side of the chin and came out through the opposite cheek. It took away several teeth and broke the jawbone. The wounded man was laid out on a table, half dazed with pain and loss of blood. Later in the day two doctors bandaged the wound and certified that he was fit to be executed. In the afternoon he was taken to the scaffold with twenty-two other outlaws. Along the road workmen jeered at the man of the maximum-wage. His turn came last and he was made to look on at the execution of his friends. As the executioner roughly tore away the bandage from his jaw he uttered a cry of pain. The hatchet dropped and put him out of his agony.

X

CONCLUSION

ROBESPIERRE'S evil reputation was made by the Thermidorian pamphleteers. In their anxiety to dissociate themselves from the best known terrorist they shifted the responsibility for their own actions upon his shoulders. Posterity believed them, because no voice rose to speak for the defence.

The conception of Robespierre as a monster will not survive the study of the numerous original documents now available. He was not bloodthirsty. Any man who shared his beliefs and who was placed in his position would have resorted to the methods he employed, and might have applied them more rigorously. He was only partly responsible for the Terror. To the end his gentler impulses struggled with his pathetic certitudes.

He was hardly a dictator and never exercised power solely by himself. He lacked the prime requisite of the dictator who does not wish to be a mere figurehead: he was not a man of action. His intelligence, penetrating, and limited, was that of a contemplative, his outlook that of a history don who has dabbled in philosophy. He would have made a fine career as a university professor, and would have resigned when Bonaparte became First Consul. Not his principles, but the fact that he was too certain of them brought him into the arena. No gladiator less suited for his task ever trod the sand. But it is a fact that for a while the public fancied the colours he sported.

The notion that Robespierre was a great, significant man will fade into thin air when it is no longer needed as an antithesis to the misconceptions that still hold the field to such a large extent. Then the unimportance of the individual called Maximilien Robespierre will be realised. The course of events was but little modified by him. He wanted freedom, equality, justice; he wanted virtue as a means towards these things, and all of them as a means towards human happiness. He endeavoured to bring them to his fellow human beings without delay. But the human material upon which he tried to work was unyielding.

Had Robespierre never existed, there would still have been a King and a Court hostile to all that was not absolutism, and ready to sell the country in order to rule it. There would still have been aristocrats loving their unfair and outmoded privileges more than their fellow-countrymen. There would still have been well-fed Jacobins spending their surplus vitality in preaching the war that ended by killing the Revolution. Had there been no Robespierre, the Hébertists and other extremists would still have been killed by the non-Girondin Jacobins afraid of communism, unless indeed the extremists had killed these Jacobins. Had there been no Robespierre, Danton might have continued to talk beautifully, to steal, to lecher and to save his country. But even this is not certain. There were other just men, savagely enamoured of virtue: Couthon, Saint-Just, and the rest. They would probably have killed Danton. As much blood would have flowed, or a little more. Perhaps, now and then, it would have spurted from different arteries.

To have changed the course of the French Revolution it would have been necessary to exclude Folly from the councils of men.

One thing would have been different, had there been no Robespierre. Among a hundred thousand opportunities one would be missing for pointing the single lesson history can teach. The lesson is that the absolute can not be wrought by men. They may dream of it, in humble uncertainty.

BIBLIOGRAPHICAL NOTE

A GOOD general introduction to the period is Brinton, C., *A Decade of Revolution* (1934), which has a highly informative bibliographical note in which the present state of the Robespierre controversy is admirably summarised. There is also an extensive bibliography. This book, like *The Jacobins* (1930), by the same author, sometimes suffers from a haste to draw conclusions and from too great a fondness for paradox.

Three general works are indispensable:

1. Aulard, *Histoire Politique de la Révolution Française, 1789-1804* (1902), where, as in the same author's *Les Orateurs de la Convention,* and in his lectures and other works upon the period, will be found the conception of a self-seeking, dishonest Robespierre and a patriotic, honestly revolutionary Danton.

2. Mathiez, A., *La Révolution Française,* 3 vols. (1922-27), gives a good notion of the newer theory of the impeccable and infallible Robespierre, social reformer and genius.

3. In the Collection 'Peuples et Civilisations,' vol. xiii., *La Révolution Française* (1930), the first part, by Lefèbvre, G., a not entirely orthodox disciple of Mathiez, attempts a synthesis of which the main lines appear acceptable to me. (Excellent bibliographies.)

The study of the French Revolution has produced more literature than that of any other period of

171

similar length in human history. It is impossible to give a complete list of authorities. No unpublished material has been used. The following brief mentions must suffice as a guide.

For the writings and speeches of Robespierre, see Lanson, G., *Manuel Bibliographique de la Littérature Française Moderne,* vol. iv. (1925), p. 679 sqq., and vol. v. (1925), p. 1664. I have used Vellay, Ch., *Discours et Rapports de Robespierre* (1908), and the two vols, of the *Œuvres Complètes,* published by the Sociéte des Études Robespierristes (1910 and 1913).

The numerous monographs of Albert Mathiez deserve special attention. They contain a wealth of hitherto unpublished material. *Robespierre Terroriste* (1921) should be read because it contains Mathiez' profession of faith. In *Autour de Danton* (1926) Mathiez tells us that if the history of the French Revolution is better studied 'it will cease to be that garden of Eden, the blessed land of heroism and virtue its patented admirers depict with so much complacency, that country of horror and crime its sworn detractors try to conjure up before us. It will appear to us what it was, multiple and varied like life, neither uglier nor finer than mankind.' Mathiez did not always live up to this ideal.

There are many biographies of the principal actors in the drama. Madelin's *Danton* (1914) shows to what extent the work of Mathiez had shaken the foundations of Danton's reputation. Only one biography of Robespierre is indispensable. It is that by

BIBLIOGRAPHICAL NOTE

Hamel, E., 3 vols. (1865, 1866, 1867); hagiographic but fully documented, with a bias so obvious that it could hardly lead the reader astray.

There are memoirs by Robespierre's sister Charlotte, which must be used with care. A critical edition has been made by Fleischmann, H., *Charlotte Robespierre et ses Mémoires* (1910). The same author's *Robespierre et les Femmes* (1909) is not without interest.

INDEX

INDEX

(1)